T0063212

The Management Opened Junior High School During The Nine Years Compulsory Programe

A Multi-Sites study
on Three Open Junior High School

SOETYONO ISKANDAR

MAKASSAR STATE UNIVERSITY
PROGRAMME PASCASARJANA
MAY 2014

authorHOUSE®

AuthorHouse™ LLC
1663 Liberty Drive
Bloomington, IN 47403
www.authorhouse.com
Phone: 1-800-839-8640

Published by AuthorHouse   08/15/2014

ISBN: 978-1-4969-3373-7 (sc)
ISBN: 978-1-4969-3372-0 (e)

CONTENTS

TABLE LIST

FIGURE LIST

ABSTRACT

Iskandar, Soetyono. 2011. *The Management opened Junior High School during the Nine Years Compulsory Programme (A Multi-Sites Study on Three Open Junior High School)*..

To generaline the access of education for Indonesian people by extending and generalizing the change of education in formal line, particularly in level of open junior high school. Besides, to extend the access for the youth of 13-15 years old, open junior high school needs extending through optimal capacity and development of the school through the model of innovative alternative education service. Therefore management of nine year compulsory education of open junior high school, the principal as the educational manager is required to perform his perserverance and skill in running the school education system.

This research applies qualitative research approach with the design of multy-sites research and applies the technique of data. Assembly through deep interview, observation and document. To coincide with the research goal, the research focus is as follow: (a) The school plan in running open Junior High School during the nine years compulsory education programme. (b) The organizing of executing open Junior High School during the nine years compulsory education programme. (c) The development of the executor source in running of open Junior High School during the nine years compulsory education programme. (d) The management audit system of open Junior High School during the nine years compulsory education programme.

Result of the research is as follows: *First*, the staff management plan should have done as the design management school. It is necessary to support the system of development and placement for the good and exact teachers and tutors. The principal needs creating conducive atmosphere in such a way that the management executor that is the teacher/tutor is involved in formulating yhe management execution and they are expected to participate proactively in contributing ideas on the operational of the school management. *Second,* The available organization basically has run well and has functioned yet as it is required, yet the ordering better system and working procedure are still needed so the coordination between the principal and the teacher/tutor internally and externally can be improved. The principal has to arrange the form/executing operational standard of each school to eliminate fragmentation. *Third,* The development of the available source needs better planning usage and improvement to support the execution more effective and efficient management. Any principal has to work hard to assure the teacher/tutor to execute management reformation for the sake of the school existence and continuance in the future. The utilization of the training result needs the support of recruitment system and teacher/tutor appointment, so there will be an obvious form/executing operational standard between the principal and teacher/tutor in selecting the needed teacher/tutor with his principal field. *Fourth,* Management audit system Improvement of the teacher/tutor competence and quality in every school. In his case, every principal has to improve the message quality that is addressed to the teacher/tutor through the comprehension of "what, why, when, where and how" about the management on the teacher/tutor competence improment so it will be more obvious. Besides, every principal needs formulating the strategic steps to advance the effectiveness of management communication to all the teachers/tutors. Further, the teacher/tutor is expected to give feed back to complete the message substance delivered by their principal. The education executor management should take the benefit of the research result as an asset to expand the school in future. Furthermore, it will be much better, if the educational execution management is supported by interscholastic in endeavoring and taking the benefit of the capital owned by the stakeholders or through the rotation pattern as what is recently performed by Directorate General of Higher Education Ministry of National Education. This can also be applied as an effort to refresh as well as to expand the teacher's/tutor's academic. Afterwards, the educational executor management with its regular method and immediate start.

The suggestions, for: (a) To government, particularly the linked deparment, the basic open Junior High School during the nine years compulsory education programme. Managed monitor and evaluate design the open Junior High School management during the nine years compulsory education programme in remote areas. By so doing, there will be some improvement and development to reach the goal as what the school, society and government hope; (b) To Provincial Education Department and Kemdinas in developing science managed organization as the theory organization in education field, especially policy science and educational development for nine year basic education; (c) The principal, particularly open Junior High School, always wanted to increased the power source the open Junior High School in order to drive the increasing of maximum achievement in the nine years compulsory education programme; (d) To other researchers, could done and traced another of this research as empirical and theoretical, might be considered as a reference for further research by applying the approach of similar hind research design, and/or the approach of different research.

Key Word: the management of Open Junior High School during the Nine Years Compulsory.

INTRODUCTION

Thank you God, for your blessing and grace since this book have written, with its title: Management Open Junior High School during The nine years compulsory programme. (Multy-Sites Study at three open Junior High School Teratai, Tulip, Mawar) could be accomplished at precisely time.

In this opportunity the writer expressed great concern regarding thank you to my: Chief Promotor (Prof. Dr. Hendyat Soetopo, M.Pd); Co-Promotor I (Prof. Dr. Marthen Pali, M.Psi); Co-Promotor II (Prof. Dr. Willem Mantja, M.Pd). Three of them was our figure as my parent with his patient and loyal that have always given its motivation, guiding, correction and suggestion.

For my darling Rita Iskandar, my daughter Margaret Iskandar, S.I.P, M.Pd, at Makassar South Celebes. Panji Sutrisno, S.E, Maya Caroline Iskandar, S.T. Grandson Nick Owen Thio at Kediri East Java, encourage without tired and prayed for me.

Finally writer could said thank you and plead to God blessed them. So that this book could be beneficial to everyone where have read and given contribute to management science develop.

Makassar May, 07 2014
Writer

CHAPTER I

Introduction

This chapter to describe about: a. research context; b. research focus; c. research goal; d. research benefit; e. term definition, f. literature study.

A. Research Context

As constitution Indonesian government in 1945 had been amandment chapter 31, those are; (1) each citizen entitle to find education, (2) each citizen compulsory to follow a base education and government due to finance, (3) government effort and make a system national education that quicken the faith afford intelligent nation life. Chapter 31 constitution Indonesian government in 1945 with encourage that each Indonesia citizen compulsory education. This things pointed that Indonesia secured and guarantee to entitle of human-being, each Indonesia citizen for affording intelligent education nation life as a goal's Indonesia. Therefore, each Indonesia citizen compulsory to follow a base education. Beside it Chapter 31 constitution Indonesian government in 1945 government due to finance a base education, with effort and evoke a sytem national education that must be acquired to guarantee average opportunity education, haul the quality with efficiency education management against the challenge in era globalization information technology and communication that immense development this time. Community education in sightful with its financed because it was very expensive. That's true expensive education made difficulty for making policy education, if government did not handle it with professional. Even that, community at the region in poverty, of course people hoped popular education or helped the people without burden for its finance. In contrast, community at the city, they intent at exclusive education with expensive finance with its reason about quality.

Based education, as its level education, that are Junior High School and college. Level education at Indonesia as; Sekolah Dasar (SD) and Madrasah Ibtidaiyah (MI), with Sekolah Menengah Pertama (SMP) and Madrasah Tsanawiyah (MTs), or the other that as a level. (Sukmadinata, (2007:255).

Extend the strategy and average opportunity education that have done by government focused at the compulsory nine years education programme, kind and others education level included with indicator out-put were; (1) mayoritas population education minimal Junior High School (SMP) and participant increased education, with extend for fields technology and superior; (2) culture learning increased at the community that total participant Junior High School (SMP) at a regular programme, as courses and community education programme; (3) quickening proportion population unfortunately have opportunity learned at all education level. (Rochaety, 2005:37).

Policy strategy planning National Education Minister in 2005-2009 pointed that rebuild national education till 2025, education for aging population in Indonesian 7-15 years man and woman could be received at formal education and integrated with inclusive education. Beside it, population age 13-15 years develop at the Open Junior High school with service model as altenative education. (Depdiknas, 2006:40).

Government region UU No. 32 Tahun 2004, in policy formulate region autonomy. Management special education as institution, curriculum, human being source, funding operational and infrastructure. So management region education more effective, and could be implementation at the region. Government role Nomor 25 Tahun 2000 have given, but could be done as the region.

Managemant education at region, Rochaety (2005:54) said one factor tahat could not be enjoyed the quality of education because management education professionally still low. Management education and commitment government for reaching the higest. Rochaety, (2005:54) said that still many between their have not experience and back ground with its education knowledge in management education. For effective the implementation must done at the principle professional in management program education.

Since 1970's government have established open junior high school at several region, and its meeting at the hall' region with several teacher/tutor have fixed to teach there. And then year 1994 government established open junior high school together with junior high school (Stuart, 2008).

At the open Junior High School during the nine years compulsory education programme, we hope principle of the school as manager. For managing open junior high school more effectively, education at the school could managed with expert and flexible. We hoped could managed all of problem processing at the open Junior High School during the nine years compulsory education programme.

The condition of Malang'education increased quality of the human being source, served average the increased of the population education. A larger composition education of the population still low, since efforted the building of education delay. The building of Malang'education efforted to increased of the quality and competence community, so their participation and function more useful and significant in building the nation. Malang'Government, (2009:11).

Open Junior High School;

> "Open Junior High School was a subsystem at Junior High School education that made the best student in learning for itself with guide from other person" Depdiknas, (2005:5).

Open Junior High School as a model alternative served education that managed from regular Junior High School. Regular Junior High School managed education with *dual system*, means served two group student with a different learning. Open Junior High School served education far distant education system for obstacle student. Operation the Open Junior High School (SMP Terbuka) have visi, misi and purpose that same with national education purpose.

B. Research Focus.

Research based context, made this research focus were; how that management Open Junior High School (SMP Terbuka) Teratai, Tulip, Mawar, during the nine years compulsory education programme at Malang region. The research focus were described at sub-focus as the next:

1. Planning about managed the Open Junior High School (SMP Terbuka) during the nine years compulsory education programme at Malang region.
2. Organization managed the Open Junior High School (SMP Terbuka) during the nine years compulsory education programme at Malang region.
3. Development management source power the Open Junior High School (SMP Terbuka) during the nine years compulsory education programme at Malang region.
4. Management audit system the Open Junior High School (SMP Terbuka) during the nine years compulsory education programme at Malang region.

C. Research Purpose

As the research focus penelitian, this research Purpose was description execution management the Open Junior High School (SMP Terbuka) Teratai, Tulip, Mawar, during the nine years compulsory education programme at Malang region. And then special this research aim, were:

1. Planning description school about management the Open Junior High School (SMP Terbuka) during the nine years compulsory education programme at Malang region.

2. Organization description management the Open Junior High School (SMP Terbuka) during the nine years compulsory education programme at Malang region.

3. Management source power development description the Open Junior High School (SMP Terbuka) during the nine years compulsory education programme at Malang region.

4. Management audit system analysis and description the Open Junior High School (SMP Terbuka) during the nine years compulsory education programme at Malang region.

D. Research Benefit

This research executed with hope could benefit to:

1. Government Malang region, in this National Education Minister at Malang region integrated with Government and based education as nine years compulsory education, the Open Junior High School (SMP terbuka) during the nine years compulsory education programme at Malang region. This research invented be hoped could considered as one of based or input in done monitoring and evaluation or assess against management the Open Junior High School (SMP Terbuka) during the nine years compulsory education programme at a far region. So that could done action repairing and developing towards accomplish an execellent gol school, community and government.

2. For Education Minister Province and National Education Minister in developing science, and this research result be hoped could be input for making policy more than that continue and develop education and for nine years compulsory.

3. For princilple, special the Open Junior High School (SMP Terbuka) during the nine years compulsory education programme at Malang region, this research result as input for monitoring and evaluation against management the Open Junior High School (SMP Terbuka) so that could increased accomplish the maximal gol management nine years compulsory education programme.

4. For others research, be hoped could be an inspiration for the research and science work and could considered as reference for that wanted to done continue this research with used approach design, and/or different approach research.

E. Term Definition

This research definison as the next;

1. That means management Open Junior High School (SMP Terbuka) was an education institution, that given opportunity to student for finishing based education.

2. Open Junior High School (SMP Terbuka) was empower community institution, its organization, included family. In its development have studied with integrated approached from education, communication, physiology, and engineering.

3. Nine years compulsory was extended and average education service for child-age, included children with special needed at the far places.

4. School was planned common action that would done at the programme of principle.

5. Organization was job description between workteam as proportional, professional in done worked at the school with full responsible and awared.

6. Development source power were as quantity and quality, at any facility physic and instrument, science laboratory, library, learning-media, infrastructure.

7. Audit system were process that included material, study, practical with activity teaching and learning (included implementation and design), assessment (worked result orientation) and quality lesson.

F. Literature Study

In this part to discuss about: i. Education Management Study; ii. Based Education Policy; iii. Open Junior High School (SMP Terbuka); iv. Open Junior High school (SMP Terbuka) Management.

I. Education Management Study

Cooper, (2004:3) described that education management as process where there is needed, aim and intensity that used inview at objective, law and programme.

Muhadjir, (2004:43), expressed that education management as effort for social problem solution to justiced and well-being community.

1. Education Management Theories

Suryadi dan Tilaar, (1994:17) said three views that develop from different thought in education management, were (a) Functionalism Theory, (b) Capital Law Theory, and (c) Empirical Theory.

a. Fungtionalism Theory

This theory given attention at empower human-being source power intellectual as effective so would given impact that a giant strength for our State. Suryadi dan Tilaar, (1994:19). With option effort and empower humankind source power as efficiency have been aim building almost all of the world state.

The first Functional Theory Amerika Serikat, Burtin Clark. Suryadi dan Tilaar, (1994:22) in this book that subject *"Educating the Expert Society"* Introduce education sociology theory that be known with *"Technological Functionalism"*. Clark described that extended education at the school not always as an one cirri education democracy. Opportunity to find education at school could extended and made more average but what a student found not same.

b. Capital Human-being Theory

Rahardjo, (1997:83) said;

"In *capital humankind theory* expressed that more higher education or skill that be accomplished by someone, most highest investagated that needed and most highest education level or skill that someone have. If come to field work, be hoped would earned that the most highest. So if happened different education level in community, therefore would happened different earned".

At 1961 and 1962 years Denison dan Schultz. Suryadi dan Tilaar, (1994:23) noticed that education given direct contribution against the growth earned State, through increased ability and skill production from work-power. The fact of this research pointed there is economy value from education.

Capital Humankind Theory was one current mind that considered that human-being as one capital as an others capital forms, for instance: technology, machine, soil, money dan as that very decided against productivity growth. Through investagated himself, someone could extended alternative for choosing profession, job or others activity for well-being life.

As theory, approached *capital humankind* decribed as an education in an increased well-being. Term *capital humankind* pointed characteristic and attribute individual that been main capital be accomplished aim someone. This included satisfied level development physic and cognitive with support health, nutrition and education. This approached emphasized that education as an important instrument to decrease poverty level through increased earned and intervention education against poverty dimension. Through approacged *capital humankind* would seen how education could be used digunakan for choosing extend that there are produktivity and the most highest income. In *capital humankind* convinced that *"knowledge - and the capacity to put knowledge to good use – is now the only dependable source of wealth all over the world."* (Suryadi dan Tilaar, 1994:24).

Tilaar, (1997:151) expressed "education have function and actor for citizen education, prepared power that have characteristic that wanted industrial work field, not as main responsible". But not means that education institution at all did not responsible against preparation job power. And then said: "that true was education put based characteristic someone job power that main needed by modern community". Therefore education must sure against claimed and needed that happened at community.

Nine years based education programme abided strategy value. This policy abided value when we integrated with efforted education development as parts from development building nation character. With policy citizen at education level that more high than Open Junior High School (SMP), with based skill average our nation to more a level. Advanced States, study compulsory integrated with law sanction. Our State study concept without jurisdiction sanction. Indonesia concept compulsory study means have prepared infrastructure and did not integrated with jurisdiction sanction but more at moral sanction that the parents careless our children. (Tilaar, 1997:152).

c. Empirism Theory

This thought based at results analysis and research' Hodgetts R. M. (1990: 138, 633) "*The American Occupational Structure*", dan "*The Equality of Educational Opportunity*," as the next;

1) Social Mobilize and Education

Study Suryadi and Tilaar, (1994:27) given our noticed against an education as instrument for bearing social level from a generation to others generation. Hodgetts R. M. in its study analysis used analysis technical statistic at theory foundation be called "*Evolutionary Functionalisms*".

In its an analysis Hodgetts R. M. conclusion that status in job not more influence generation factor but must be proved through prestige that recognizable as extended so happened thought from *ascription* to thought *achievement*.

2) Education Opportunity Equality

In concept education equality did not constant and difficult given a distinct understood. Suryadi and Tilaar, (1994:29) distinction three concept equality, were;

(a) The thoughts given the same our treatment that based group criterion that could been received consider same.

(b) Treatment that as for founding result that equality or near one with the others.

(c) Competed must have recognized community with the same level.

Management towards average early with efforted added schools. Study directly at management equality education that have studied by Robin Reiter. Invented that very important in study Robin Reiter was output in a different between conceptional average in a passive education, with average active education. (Suryadi and Tilaar, 1994:34).

Passive equality education more emphasized at an equality founded opportunity for listing at the school, active average was the same opportunity that school have given to student that listed so found the higher result.

Miarso, Y. (2007) with "*Equality of Educational Opportunity*", described that equality problem opportunity education around at five things, were: (1) because rasio regression opportunity did not equality, (2) because tangible input source did not equality at school system, (3) because source that decreased tangible moral teacher did not equality, (4) did not average input compared with effectively result study, (5) did not equality result study as a proved that fact would not equality opportunity. Miarso, Y. (2007) in his study at Chili about "*Eight Tear of Their Life Through Schooling to the Labor Market*". This study expressed as an concept education equality that more comprehensive than conception equality that been used Robin Reiter. As this concept equality of educational opportunity not only limit at whwt the student abided the same opportunity inside the school, but more than it.

Equality concept education as Suryadi and Tilaar, (1994:32) cover; "First, equality of access that education founded, second equality of survival at the school, third, equality of output in learning, and fourth, equality of outcome education.

Miarso, (1985:49) "develop awared equality opportunity education, as abased for democracy community, where each community member more awared where our compulsory". Have many effort that have done from scientist equality definition education opportunity and criteria community as indicator level output. *Havighurst* as quoted by Miarso, (1985) prompt a suggest so that "indicator equality from opportunity that have given to student with certainly intellectual skill (example Junior High School/SMP)".

Therefore described that equality education not the same education, but the same attention, so all student could develop maybe a good person and maximum.

3) Economy Growth and Education

Suryadi and Tilaar, (1994:34) at our study about economy growth United States (Amerika Serikat) invented that education contributed against growth *output* about 15% from Schultz also have done education contributed indicator against economy growth with used analysis technic *rate of return.*

Schultz'indicator compared rate of return to humankind capital with rate of return to physical capital. Education output invented from growth level *output* at USA caused education as one investigation power source humankind development.

Denison expressed his study that the education contributed variety at the advanced States begin the low, were "Jerman (2%) and the highest Kanada (25%). Asian, education contributed average against economy growth enough high and continent Africa'States, the most highest average." (Suryadi dan Tilaar, 1994:33).

Rate of return education Indonesia each level not yet high. Any study that have done expressed that Achmady, (1994:30) *rate of return* education were; 0,10-0,20 for SD; 0,16 for SMP; 0,16-0,32 for SMU; 0,16-0,22 for Diploma Programme and 0,13-0,21 Sarjana level.

World Bank Study Suryadi and Tilaar, (1994:35) that have done by Jamison and Lau at 1982 year have invented that: "Investigated develop seed, irrigation, and used manure evident more productive *output* plantation if have been done with the farmer that have studied at SD compared with farmers without education".Output study that have done by Jamison and Lau this pointed education urgent for community. Therefore the education needed to give as average and equality.

Prasetyo, (2007:105), in his research expressed, formal education as strategies in economy building. Without education, would established obstacle economy building. Through pedagogy human would equally the relevant values with economy building. Buchori, (2001:7) expressed that each nation that true wanted to prepare himself for the future, must brave made changes in his education system, although formal education and non-formal education. Extended and equality opportunity found based education.

II. Based Education Policy and Compulsory

1. Based Education foundation Policy and Compulsory

Policy or rule that managed operasional compulsory based education Depdiknas, (2005: 8-14), included;

(a) Ideal foundation, Pancasila as based or foundation in managed nasional building.
(b) Constitution; UU 1945: 1) Opened UUD 1945, alinea IV "…for intelligence nations life.…", 2) Chapter XIII Verse 31 ayat: (a) Each citizen to be found education, (b) Government efforted and manage national education system that have managed at the rules.
(c) Operational Foundation

Operational foundation building State included education was Decidedness People Representation Committee (MPR) about State Direction Big Lined (GBHN). GBHN called operational foundation because have given a big lines about activity that must do be accomplish nation and State building as a purpose, liked at Pancasila and UUD 1945. At our reformation, this State Direction Big Lined (GBHN) changed with Midle Distance Build Planned. Others was education system rule, President Instruction and Minister Rule.

Though national education operational foundation at expedient compulsory study were as the next;

1. Decision Decidedness People Representation Committee (MPR) RI No. II/MPR/1993, to increase quality human-being power source. Education Departemen and Culture Decision theme of subject policy for Pelita VI, were; (1) education opportunity equality, (2) education relevance with building, (3) education quality, and (4) management efficiency.

2. Constitution No. 20 Tahun 2003, about National Education System, this rules legitimated at 8 Juli 2003. This constitution as a changed constitution No. 2 1989 year about National Education System. As constitution No. 20 Tahun 2003, function national education was for developing skill and forming character with nation culture that intelligence in nation life intelligent. National education purposed were student potency development so to be human-being that faithful to The God, exalted, healthy, knowledged, smart, creative, self-government, and to be citizen that democracy and responsible Depdiknas, (2003). Compared with Constitution No. 2 1989 year, Constitution Nomor 20/2003 loaded many new rule especially that supported aspect acquire, recreation and spread knowledge. In constitution Republic Indonesia Nomor 20 Tahun 2003 about National Education System; (1) Chapter VIII, verse 34 as the next;

   (1) Each citizen that six years old could compulsory programme study skill finished based education.

   (2) Government and Government region guarantee compulsory management study minimal at based education level without fee.

   (3) Compulsory study as responsible State that managed by Education Institution, Government, Government region and Community.

   (4) Appointment about verse (a), verse; (b) be managed more with Government Rule. (Depdiknas, 2003).

3. Permendiknas Nomor 35 Tahun 2006, about Accelaration National Movement Nine years compulsory study, that expressed extend and education equality consisted; (1) extended and education serviced equality for child-ages, included with child special

needed especially the far, isolation, and behind region, (2) given a special noticed to build, give technical accessory, and subsidize to regions that its lowest earned, especially that still under 75%, and regions that absolutely high point (childless study). (Depdiknas, 2006).

2. Based Education Opportunity Equality.

Education equality include two important aspect were *equality* and *equity*. *Equality* means opportunity equality to found education, as *equity* means equity to be accomplish that same education opportunity between any community group. Access against education that equality means all population school-ages have accomplished education opportunity, as that access against education have equity if between group could have the same education. (Suharsaputra, (2008).

In relationship with euqqlity education, thus concept equality relation means that each person have opportunity and access that be accomplished education without different time, sex, social status, variety or geography location. Thus different opportunity to be accomplish education caused bu back ground student must be as small as. (Achmady, 1994:57) expressed;

"Seen from more large, equality opportunity and behavior as equity at student that different its back ground, as at the based education concept, have aspect equality more than economy social. With its access that same to be accomplish based education between chidren that different back ground economy social and its geography, thus reality based education as efforted decreased poverty …"

Efforts that have done to decrease the different or to diminish level, needed based at equity as others dimension from equality. Each efforted decreased level means equity or given that equity and exact to each person that based our back ground and condition life.

Djojonegoro (1996:86) expressed "Nine years compulsory education in an Indonesia have concept Universal basic education," that opened as extended opportunity for all student or chidages nine years compulsory education to accomplish education.

At the same source expressed that nine years compulsory education in an Indonesia have cirri; (1) unforced but persuasive, (2) not law sanction, and that more than were parent morak aspect and student build so have come to follow basuc education because anykind easily have prepared, (3) irregular with its constitution, (4) indicator output with based education participant point that more increased.

3. Audit Process at Nine Years Compulsory Education Programme.

For supporting acceleration nine years compulsory education programme, there are several efforted that Government have done. As National Education Minister (Mendiknas) declaration. Sukriswandari, (2005:59) that have five a new broken-through at nine years compulsory education.

First, supported all student after sixth class (VI SD/MI) continue to Junior High School (SMP/MTs/setara) at 2008/2009 year.

Second, done through the region seeked-for child-ages (13-15 years) after finished sixth class (SD.MI/Sederajat), but not yet to continue to Junior High School (SMP/MTs/Sederajat) and chil *drop out* (DO) SMP/MTs/Sederajat to come at the school.

Third, prepared anykind design education and support infrastructure, tough as power source, infrastructure, and financial education to support a new student 2008/2009 year.

Fourth, used programme a new school unit (USB), a new class-room (RKB), and SD-SMP together at 2008 for receiving a new student 2008/2009.

Fifth, ope house till September 2008 to receive a new student Open Junior High School (SMP Terbuka) and register student for programme B package. "Register time till September so can reach a target 95 %", said National education Minister (Mendiknas). Programme Implementation Judgement with *Process-Audit*

1. Audit Understand

The common audit as an evaluation process that result a judgement. The American Accounting Association auditing definition as; "*A systematic process of objectively obtaining and evaluating evidence regarding assertions about economic action and events to ascertain the degree of correspondence between these assertion and established criteria and communicating the result to interested users.*" (Schawandt & Halpen, 1988:19).

Audit purpose was found and evaluation evidence empirical that integrated with claim against actions and events as economy for knowing grade relation between the claim with criteria that have fixed and comunication to interconnect the results. Thus, have said that benefit audit was as control instrument against at an activity, include education activity.

Audit was rechecked that reconstructive and comprehensive as accurate through strategy *Reflective and Evaluative Document* (RED). University of Nottingham, (2002). Components learning that have audited were (1) material learning although theory study or practical included as purpose, (2) process, at activity of *teaching and learning* (although design or implementation), and (3) assessment (work result orientation) and (4) lesson quality.

Procedure audit used the steps as the next; (1) preparation of a plan of study; (2) internal and external fact-finding; (3) content analysis; (4) development of conclusions and recommendations; and (5) communication of the result of the audit.

Approach *process-Audit* this used quality method, this method fasten for evaluative research type that process given *judgement* against curriculum implementation that would added capacity management education. *Process-Audit* in this research have placed in perspective research whole scientific, thus *process-Audit* included at pragmatism.

Although audit type that the other was *pre-audit* at the commom, have done against *desk-evaluation*, *process-audit* as reconstruction process, and *post-audit* as *sustainability* after done audit.

2. Audit frame taught in Education Programme Management Assessment.

Approach audit have used in the world an education since 1990-s through management *Program-based Competitive Funding,* Competition Present Programme for increasing work and capacity college at the State. Competition Present Programme for increasing academic community awared for increasing worker and capacity education programme.

Process-Audit in an education have done at several State, as; Jepang, Australia, Yordania, Inggris, Finlandia, and Thailand in aspect teaching, learning, assessment, monitoring, and factor others supported. The component have audited as internal with used strategy *Reflective and Evaluative Document* (RED). (University of Nottingham, 2005).

During this monitoring against management Government Counsellor Professional Education done through evaluation external (accreditation) by Government more in an administrative, means evaluation done to programme study start from programme study self-evaluation, *site visit,* till last certainly value that as score. Score academic assessment, not deep, seldom ignore "why" from management process was used the programme. Programme evaluation by accessor in accreditation process have done for testing valid and advantage the programme. A colleague-evaluation with "*Process-Audit*" have done as Quality Care at counsellor study programme and learning. (Raka Joni, 1989)

Accreditation and *Process-Audit* both have the same unsure in *Star-point* was prepared *self-evaluation* programme, in contrast both with different purpose or target. Accreditation done at efforted self-evaluation assessment against study programme work by accessor.

Asesor assessment result always visitation as agreement (although less or more study programme work) as report to the study programme principle. Different with assessment at the process and accreditation (that there are repaired the work that have done by that assessment, because interconnected with commitment finanace used). Obviously could said that research used *Process-Audit,* done at the quality-care. Counsellor learning programme assessed indirect for repairing the work.

Sidi, (2001:93), program essential in the nine years compulsory wrere; (a) build infrastructure; (b) received the new teacher so have enough teacher; (c) bought quality lesson book and reached the rasio student and the book'useful = 1:1; (d) done a special education social safety net programme for poverty family student; (e) coordination vertical and horizontal; and (f) involve all strength participant.

From both ideas could be taken the conclusion that factors could be supported the nine years compulsory education programme;

   a. Government policy that priority education sector, prominent that interconnected with eduction infrastructure, education finance and education power.
   b. Included community unsure at tha nine years compulsory education.
   c. Education decentralization, but must have integerted between centre government policy with government regional.

Though that obstacle in managed the nine years compulsory education programme, were:

   a. Condition geography of Indonesia as island State made difficult to extend education serviced.
   b. The limited education infrastructure, so not yet could able made unit chil-ages.
   c. Less education power and teacher.
   d. Stiil there are family lived underline the poverty, so all the member's family must be worked to fill-up their needed living everyday. Sukriswandari, (2005:60).

Sidi, (2001:91), problem that against the nine years compulsory education were;

   a. Less infrastructure for student Junior High School (SMP), especially at the village, the far region, the border region.
   b. Highest point drop out of the student.
   c. The low quality basic education.
   d. The low of community group participant in supporting compulsory education, as consequence geography obstacle, culture and economy at the placed.
   e. Coordination in activity special compulsory education at the region never done effectively.

III. Open Junior High School (SMP Terbuka)

1. Understanding Open Junior High School (SMP Terbuka)

"Open Junior High school (SMP Terbuka) was an education subsystem at the level Junior High School (SMP) that prominent the student learning by self with a limit counsel from others." (Depdiknas, 2005:5).

Open Junior High School (SMP Terbuka) as a model alternative education serviced at level Junior High School (SMP) that managed by Junoir High School regular (SMP regular). Open Junior Highy School (SMP Terbuka) not institution or the new technical manage unit that establish by itself, but followed at the Junior High School regular (SMP reguler) that have operationed. Junior High School regular (SMP reguler) as the mother managed education with *dual system model*, meants (two in one) two group serviced student that different, with different of learning. Jnuior High School (SMP) managed Open Junior High School (SMP Terbuka) as the based extend or added work, as an education serviced with open far distance system that for student that have certain obstacle. Open Junior High School'Student have serviced education through self-learning system. In its operational Open Junior High School (SMP Terbuka) have vision, mission and purpose that harmonious national education purpose.

2. Open Junior High School (SMP Terbuka) Vision and Mission

Vision that Open Junior High School (SMP Terbuka) education system part were "quality output, selfies and responsible with extended goal involved." (Depdiknas, 2005:6). As the mision was education alternative created that able extended community opportunity learning, followed community learning all the life, and development self-attitude in learning. With the mission, Open Junior High School (SMP Terbuka) serviced output Junior School especially that ages 13-15 years or maximal 18 years that unfortune because economy social condition, transportation facility limited, geography condition or against obstacle time, impossible they followed as student Junior High School regular (SMP regular) lesson.

3. Open Junior High school (SMP Terbuka) Purpose

Open Junior High School (SMP Terbuka)' pupose same with Junior High School regular (SMP reguler)'purpose, was; "given able based provision that as extend with increased knowledge and skill that have at the Junior School that benefit for the development life self-student, community members, and citizen as with the development level and prepared student for living in community and/or followed the next education to Junior High School (SMP)." Depdikbud, (1993).

Beside it Open Junior High School (SMP Terbuka) also development with purpose for all output Junior School (SD) that because geography condition and obstacle economy social studied to Junior High School (SMP) regular and a design to support management compulsory based education (Dikdas) nine years. (Depdiknas, 2005:7). With where there are Open junior High school (SMP Terbuka) be hoped as extended opportunity have education service that could done and quality.

The purpose as toward for principal as managed Open Junior High School (SMP Terbuka) in used the concepts Open Junior high School (SMP Terbuka) at the field. Management Open Junios High School (SMP Terbuka) have said to yield if the purposes have reached. The purposes as reduction sustain from vision and mision Open Junior High School (SMP Terbuka) and as united that could not separated one and others. So obviously relation between vision and mission, and the purpose above noticed figure the next;

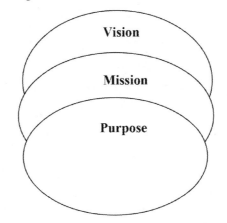

Figure 1.1 Relationship between vision, mission and purpose Open Junior high School (SMP Terbuka) (Depdiknas, 2005:8)

4. Open Junior High School Management Foundation

a. Philosophy Foundation

Development Open Junior High School (SMP Terbuka) have based as consideration. Consideration above philosophy foundation, theory foundation, and constitutional foundation. Consideration various the foundation could be as based to find the right study so could fixed as science discipline that establish itself. For explaining philosophy foundation Open junior High

School (SMP Terbuka) system, there are three factors that needed be study were consideration ontology, epistemology, and aksiology. Depdiknas, (2005:9), sebagai berikut:

First, ontology consideration have managed at Open Junior High School (SMP Terbuka), were based at postulate that human-being was borned in a different condition, have able to develop as self-different, able to develop with genetics potence and the environmental, with have discharged to change and form individual.

While, that education and learn continue at all life, and the empiris fact still enough many population school-ages especial at Indonesia not yet and or did found education and learn through education regular system. With the postulate, could conclusion that at open education and distance far was given possible alternative education with different able to and human-being condition that coherency.

Second, epistemology consideration Open Junior High School (SMP Terbuka) as the answered about how this education system pendidikan could managed. Open Junior High school (SMP Terbuka) management with empower community institution, that have organization, include family. In the development have study with integrated approach from education, communication, physiology, and engineering. The studied have done at all and systematic begin from analysis, design, develop, management, and evaluation. In the studied to effort there is sinergity effect from various approach so collected from various the approach have added value and or more than total only. Remember that the different community potency, therefore impossible to fix a standar that have done for all community. The standard model was so all the student able to develop possible maximal as with the characteristic and limited with used potency that in its the environmental.

Third, aksiology consideration as benefit management Open Junior high School (SMP Terbuka), were student possible folowed education as with its condition and their needed. Through Open Junior High School (SMP Terbuka) student could managed each day activity as helping their parents work for their life. Student able to learn their-self between their activity that have planned for its needed. If there are problem in the learning that could not solved their-self, they could seek for helping resoucer their counsellor that neat from their or that given task for counseling.

b. Theory Foundation

That learnt have said to yield if changed from the student. Transformed as yield from a constant learnt activity and only will happen if student done the learning process by their-self. Without learning experience, the student impossible have transformed, although knowledge, skill, and attutide. (Depdiknas, 2005:11).

So could happened learning process, must be happened interaction between student with source learning. Source learning manu kind, not from a person only. Student could done learning activity although no person that teach their, prepared various source learning as book, material, instrument, technical, and environmental.

As conceptual, Open junior High School (SMP Terbuka) as education system that as possible as avoid limited or given independent to the student in learning process. At Open Jnuior High School (SMP Terbuka) each individual given independent for managing the learning process as with the condition and requisites.

Independent of open education system pendidikan and distance far as Open Junior High School (SMP Terbuka) was in used various learning source as more independent. With Self-learning system that have done, though each student could learnt everywhere and whenever without depend at the teacher/tutor. Student could learnt their-self with used any learning source beside teacher, as modul, radio programme, video programme, or others media. The various media special design so that could the student learnt by their-self. Beside function for studing lesson material, the learning-media also efforted could changed as a teacher example; organization, counsel, motivation, evaluation, and given in contras, and others.

Perscriptive Learnt Theory Frame that expression Reigeluth. Depdiknas, (2005:12) expressed there are three variables leant that intergrated, were; learnt condition, learnt behavior, and Learnt output. This theory frame could showed as the next;

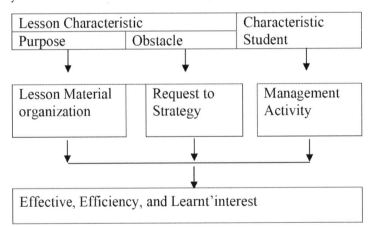

Figure 1.2 Perscriptive Learnt Theory Frame. (Depdiknas, 2005:12)

In Open Junior High School (SMP Terbuka)'concept, condition variable as output Junior SSchool (SD/MI) that have obstacle, behavior variable as learnt system that different (non-konvensional), as output variable could done for child-obstacle education. As this theory prescriptive expressed that "so student that have opportunity for continuing its education, then they needed to give a special action. (Depdiknas, 2005:12).

With learnt system that have done at Open Junior High School (SMP Terbuka) means for giving special action that different with student regular, so possible student that obstacle could continue its education. Because we hoped students that obstacle have a fix learn opportunity, then must there are learnt system non-konvensional that could covered theirs. Learnt system at Open Junior High School (SMP Terbuka) be hoped able to do it things.

c. Constitutional Foundation

Constitutional foundation management Open Junior High School (SMP Terbuka), Depdiknas, (2005:13) was as the next;

1. Opened constitution (UUD) 1945 that Indonesia expressed education purpose for intelligence nation life.

2. Chapter 31 constitution (UUD) 1945 that expressed each citizen must found education. Government be obliged to manage a national learnt system.

3. Constitution (UUUD)

    a) Constitution (UUD) No. 25 Tahun 2000 about National Build Programme 2000-2004 expressed that towards National Education Build Policy were, "efforted to extend and equity opportunity have done education that high quality for all Indonesia people …".

    b) Constitution (UUD) No. 20 Tahun 2003 about National Education System chapter 31, expressed that (1) far distance education could managed at line, level and education type, (2) far distance education it function given education serviced to community group that did not followed regular education, (3) far distance education managed in any form, modul, and cover that supported by infrastructure and learnt serviced also assessment system that guarantee quality output as education national standard.

Beside covered at the constitution foundation, management Open junior High school (SMP Terbuka) based operational foundation National Educational Departement (Depdiknas) also, (2005:14), as;

1. Kep. Menko Kesra No. 01 Tahun 1989 about nine years compulsory education.

2. Kepmen Dikbud No. 034/U/1979 tanggal 21 Februari 1979 about the first Open Junior High School (SMP Terbuka) at five location.

3. Kepmen Dikbud No. 54/U/1993 about Junior High School (SMP).

5. Characteristic, Component, and Organization Open Junior High School (SMP Terbuka).

a. Characteristic Open Junior High School (SMP Terbuka)

Open Junior High School (SMP Terbuka) have common characteristic, Depdiknas, (2005:15) as the next;

First, Open Junior High School (SMP Terbuka) as education line formal school level Junior High school (SMP) and as part integral from institution Junior High school (SMP) as their mother. With Open Junior High School (SMP Terbuka) not as institution or New Technical Managed Unit, beside it a education serviced form that managed by Junior High School regular (SMP Reguler) that have done.

Second, its learnt activity have done open/far distance education system, so student have done learnt activity theirself. Therefore its process learnt managed more independent and given opportunity that more extend student for controlling it learnt activity. Student have given opportunity to fix the time, placed and learnt activity as able to and each needed.

Third, used curriculum and quality standard the common that have done Junior High School (SMP), so student and output Open Junior High School (SMP Terbuka) have obligation and that same compentence with Junior High School regular (SMP reguler). Student main lesson material Open Junior High School (SMP Terbuka) as a printed modul and supported with others media, as audio caset, video, transparantion, and sources that at around environmental. Practical activity have done, student Open Junior High School (SMP Terbuka) used laboratorium, Language, skill room, Art room, library and others that there are at the mother Junior High School (SMP).

For increasing knowledge and skill student that integrated with capability life, Open Junior High School (SMP Terbuka) develop skill that as the skill around theirs. Each placed could different skill that development.

Fourth, Open Junior High School (SMP Terbuka) empower that power at Junior High School regular (SMP reguler), although principal, teacher/tutor, administration. Means, have not a new power education for managing Open Junior High School (SMP Terbuka). Beside empower from Junior High School regular (SMP Reguler) and Open Junior High School (SMP Terbuka) used teacher/tutor lived around theirs.

b. Component Open Junior High School (SMP Terbuka)

Component Open Junior High School (SMP Terbuka) not different with component at Junior High School regular (SMP reguler), were student component, curriculum, learnt material, learnt activity, learnt infrastructure, teacher/tutor, and learnt evaluation. As the components Depdiknas, (2005:17), as the next;

1. Student

Student Open Junior High School (SMP Terbuka) wasd output Junior School (SD/MI), or student drop out from Junior High School (SMP/MTs). Limit student-ages and others pre-requisites as with that have done at Junior High School regular (SMP reguler). Student Open Junior High School (SMP Terbuka) was part at the Student Junior High School regular (SMP reguler) that its mother.

2. Curriculum

Curriculum Open Junior High School (SMP Terbuka) used curriculum Junior High School (SMP) that common have done. The curriculum then be made based design Teach Learn Activity for Open Junior High School (SMP Terbuka). This based Teach Learn Activity the same contained with Lesson Programme Big Lines for school regular. The Teach Learn Activity used as model in develop material and learnt media belajar Open Junior High School (SMP Terbuka).

3. Learnt Material

Main learnt material at Open Junior High School (SMP Terbuka) was printed material as modul, that design as special so student could learnt their-self. Beside modul, at Open junior High School (SMP Terbuka) also used support learnt material as audio programme, video/VCD and others media.

4. Learnt Activity

Common activity learnt at Open Junior High School (SMP Terbuka) could different into two were learnt activity their-self and tutorial. Learnt activity at Open Junior High School (SMP Terbuka) used their-self learnt system with learnt principles finish. Student have done learnt their-self activity although as individual or group at learnt activity placed. Their-self learnt activity at their placed guiding and managing by teacher/tutor. Beside that, teacher/tutor taught activity. Their–self learnt activity and group at their placed made a learning schedule that proportional coordinate time in curriculum and difficulty level and how important the lesson. Although, this learning schedule did not as the regular school. Schedule Open Junior High School (SMP Terbuka) more as a student could arranged time for learning as more proportional. Learning strategy that to be performed when tutorial different with regular school, because more help and guide solved student difficult learning that not yet resolved at their placed. Quality guarantee output student, school also could brought tutorial as intensive at final test semester or national final test.

Arranged activity tutorial at the mother of Junior High School (SMP) that have agreed by principal dan vice, teacher/tutor. The activity tutorial become teacher/tutor task.

5. Learnt Infrastructure

a) Learnt Activity Placed

The principle student Open Junior High School (SMP Terbuka) could learnt where and when their's wanted. Although learnt student facility their-self, to be formed at special palce for doing learnt activity that called "Learnt Activity Placed" (LAP). At LAP this student group come for doing learnt activity their-self with their tutorial. Location LAP made near the student lived. LAP usually used building that there are near their placed, likes building Junior High School (SMP), the house of population, hall region, Mosque or others that possible. Each Open Junior High School (SMP Terbuka) have several LAP that the location were spread with the student'condition. (UNESCO ASPnet School).

b) Facility for Activity Tutorial

Beside learning activity at LAP, student also have given tutorial by lesson teacher from the mother school. For managing this tutorial used facility that there are at the mother school or that prepared at the environmental. When student learnt at the mother school student could used facility that the mother school have as laboratorium, skill practical instrument, library, sport infrastructure and others. Others Facility that could used at the mother school as instruments programme media supporting as OHP, video/VCD *player*. If student impossible come to the mother school, tutorial also done with system teacher coming. Means teacher come to learning activity that have known. So student that follow tutorial out the mother school could used learning facility from the mother school, when the teacher come with several learning facility from the mother school that possible. (Abdullah:2004)

c) Others Modul and Media

Almost all open education system and far distance that have used their-self learnt system involved Open Junior High School system (SMP Terbuka), print modul as main media for student learnt their-self. In development this print modul the material always followed to curriculum Junior High School (SMP) that have done, involved the contain expert (lecturer) from any College, writer that all the excellent teachers from any lesson, and learnt development. The learnt Modul also developed at the based their-self principle learnt, the concepts methodical and sustainable learnt system. Open Junior High School (SMP Terbuka) modul consist of four component, were; (a) teacher-guiding, (b) student activity book, (c) modul final test collected, and (d) modul.final test collected and key.

For completing print media at Open Junior High school system (SMP Terbuka) prepared also others media as audio, radio programme, video/ VCD player, modul integrated with audio, and media with other learnt source that there are at student environmental. The other media function for obviously all the concepts, fact, procedure, and meta cognitive that still not clear if have read with print modul. beside that for student knowledge and skill at the lesson concepts and procedure physic, biology. Open Junior High School (SMP Terbuka) scheduled done practical with used laboratorium and sport infrastructure that there are at the mother Junior High School (SMP).

6. Power

Power at the level Open Junior High School (SMP Terbuka) involved: Principal, Vice, Teacher/Tutor, Counsellor and Administration. a. Principal Open Junior High School (SMP Terbuka) was the principal of the mother Junior High School (SMP) that managed Open Junior High School (SMP Terbuka), because as institution Open Junior High School (SMP Terbuka) not as technical managed unit that established their-self, then Principal of Junior High School (SMP) as the mother also to be Principal of Open Junior High School (SMP Terbuka); b. Vice Open Junior High School (SMP Terbuka) appointment the teacher of the mother school and not double job as vice regular school. Vice this school managed all principal job at the Open Junior High School (SMP Terbuka); c. Teacher was lesson teacher at the mother school that done student learnt activity Open Junior High School (SMP Terbuka) as lesson that their teached. Main task teacher was management learnt activity tutorial; d. Tutor was community member that have given task for guiding student learnt activity at the placed (LAP). Each LAP have tutor that come from the teacher of the school or prominent community at their placed; e. Tutor was community environment LAP that have skill. Specialist Tutor usually from prominent religion, business, arts, sports that have special skill; g. Guiding teacher an Conseling that teached at the

Junior High School regular (SMP reguler); f. Administration, Open Junior High School (SMP Terbuka) used several person from the mother school that given task managed administration Open Junior High School (SMP Terbuka). (Abdullah:2004)

7. Learnt Evaluation

Learnt evaluation that managed at Open Junior High School (SMP Terbuka) involved their-self test, modul final test, unit final test, semester final test and national final test. a. tes their-self, have done each learnt activity final at the modul. After student finish learning a learnt activity, student could done problem that have prepared and could correction their-self its answer with used the answer key that have prepared; b. modul final test, each student was finished one modul that test have done for it. modul final test problem as component from the modul. Eah modul have problem set and its final test. Management modul final test was the teacher'responsible as its lesson. This modul final test could as same as formative test or daily test at Junior High School regular (SMP reguler); c. unit final test, that tes managed after student learnt the modul unit. Making problem and managed modul final test as teacher lesson responsibility. This unit final test could managed if enabled; d. semester final test, test that managed at each last semester for indicator output student during a semester. Problem material and time managed semester final test usually same with the mother school; e. ujian national examination, examination that managed for third years student at lesson last year. National final examination result used for resolving what student have considered fulfill requisites academic for passing fromOpen Junior High School (SMP Terbuka). Appointment managed national final test match with the ruler of goverment. (Fattah, 2008:107)

Mechanism managed activity have done by principal at three sites, the essence pointed that between sites that one with others have designed and strategy that same. Only its emphasized at each different site, with tutor managed each time. Encompass tutor in managed at three sites, could pointed as activity with at each criteria. Integrated tutor in management would used, although more difficulty in learnt process either managed class. (Abullah:2004)

Ross, T. (1998) commonly essential from education that have planned, organization, source power, management audit. That included planning at curriculum Open Junior High School (SMP Terbuka) that its contained same with Teaching Program Big Lines; learnt material Open Junior High School (SMP Terbuka) was print material as modul that special design; learnt activity placed Open Junior High School (SMP Terbuka) at the principle when and where only. Organization at Junior High School regular (SMP reguler) as the mother from Open Junior High School (SMP Terbuka) given a good placed; power source that's; principal, teacher/tutor, administration, and student; audit with monitoring from principal, supervisor, from teacher/tutor serviced and evaluation and national examination.

Planned an education management very important, with made with a short distance for a while and a long distance. From decision that have made and said to community, so could be considered at the school. (Arie P, 1988).

c. Open Junior High School (SMP Terbuka) Administration and Organization

1. School Operational Organization

Open Junior High School (SMP Terbuka) institution as form formal school that the mother at Junior High School (SMP) nearer that fulfill requisites. Sure organization structure Open Junior High School (SMP Terbuka) a little different with Junior High School regular (SMP reguler), because there are unsure that likes teacher/tutor. The teacher have a function as a responsible about planning and teaching managed activity at Open Junior High School (SMP Terbuka), especially tutorial teaching activity. Tutor guided learning activity at the learnt activity placed. Tutor have task about planning and developing learning activity that used environmental as learn source. Sure learning programme through environmental'use as e-learning source to each Open Junior High School (SMP Terbuka) and different placed one to another. Organization structure Open Junior High School (SMP Terbuka) could image as the next;

Education organization begun planning identification, school schedule and serviced design with a good strategy, from principal, teacher/tutor and administration that proactive. (Devlin L, 1989).

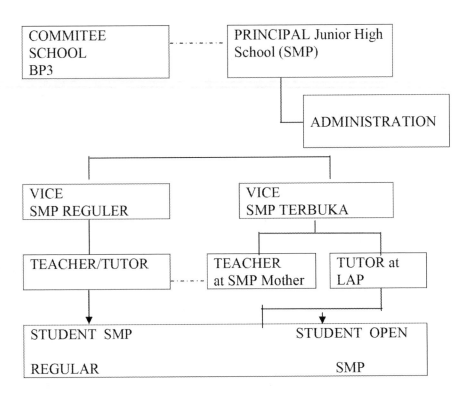

Figure 1.3 Organization Structure Junior High School Regular (SMP regular),
Open Junior High School (SMP Terbuka) (Depdiknas, 2005:25).

Power there are at Open Junior High School (SMP Terbuka) were Principal, Vice, Teacher/Tutor and Administration with others.

2. Open Junior High School (SMP Terbuka) Administration

The common Open Junior High School (SMP Terbuka) administration different with Junior High School regular (SMP reguler), consist of student administration, infrastructure administration, academic administration and finance administration. Administration at LAP involved all of administration with its job, were administration about learnt difficut, student learnt advanced, and administration distribution and useful learnt material (modul, caset, and supporting book). Therefore Open Junior High School (SMP Terbuka) its mother at Junior High School regular (SMP reguler), thus their student also as administrative register as student Junior High School mother (SMP Induk). So that student found serviced administration from Junior High School mother (SMP Induk).

Principal, teacher/tutor, administration as power source, needed approach as individual. So could formed a united team in work together, accomplished vision and mision. (Patricia N, 1987)

IV. Management Open Junior High School (SMP Terbuka)

1. Management Understanding

Sergiovanni, (1987) said: that management where administrative have done by principal consist of activities that purpose towards, so that all stakeholder involved at school worked as the school'purposed that wanted to accomplish. Management edukative as activity that towards and guide each teacher/tutor, so that managed the lesson task as right and accurate. Principal as administrator emphasized at procedure and result in an empower power source that there are for accomplishing the purpose of the school, as leader aspect emphasized at *renewal and change* and focus at *humankind interactions* for influenced others accomplish the organization purposed.

With others said, principle from principal was balanced between managerial and education leader. This two ideas (administor and leader) as *balance and support* between one with others.

Learning that have done by teacher/tutor, foremost could given a situation where student could develop competence optimal their-self as built and intellectual each student. This situation could done if teacher/tutor given to manage their class as characteristic at each lesson, student characteristic, and assessment as development each student. In the classroom teacher/tutor must done any inovation and creatifity learning, menaged class, classroom, infrastructure.

Open Junior High School management (SMP Terbuka) was education institution that managed power source at education as effective, efficiency, and responsible, and given opportunity student take finished their based education. Several management component at activity as the next; planning, organization, develop, audit. The fourth components done in rotation. This things have done as with situation and condition field, so that could result the good one. At the formularized and done with accurate, thus result education management could as with the hoped purpose.

Management eductio have meant that wide was regulations or management that involved; design, accomplishment and directors about human-being power source (student, teacher/tutor, parent and user education), curriculum and financial with education facility, for accomplishing education purpose that optimal as effective and efficiency, and how made to follow all of accomplish education purpose that the agreement. (ISPI, 1995:69).

The Rule National Education Minister Republic Indonesia Nomor 19 Tahun 2007 about Standar Education Management by Based Education Unit and Middle. Depdiknas, (2007), that each education unit obligated fulfill education management national standard. Education management standard means was involved; programme design, job sheet management, supervision and evaluation.

With management Open Junior High School (SMP Terbuka) could as process accomplished the function basic of education management at unit Open Junior High School (SMP Terbuka), were; accomplish job programmer design, supervision and evaluation. Therefore principal as manager at school have task and responsible in accomplish the basic function education management. Accomplishment the task, principal not worked theirself but have helped by vice, teacher/tutor and others staff. Principal have made job description for all their staff for accomplishing their task with responsible, and managed the accomplishment as effective and efficiency for accomplishing education advance at school as the hoped of the purpose.

2. Programme Design

Management Open Junior High School (SMP Terbuka) have done good with as the programme. Things that needed considering in the programme design itu. Depdikbud, (1992:6-8), were;

a. Mother School

Open Junior High School (SMP Terbuka) at the Junior High School regular (SMP regular) or others that have requisites as the next; 1. Principal that able to manage Junior High School regular (SMP reguler) and Open Junior High School (SMP Terbuka); 2. Vice and Teacher/Tutor must be able to do the task as daily leader at Open Junior High School (SMP Terbuka); 3. Teacher/Tutor that able to do the added task at the Open Junior High School (SMP Terbuka); 4. Administration could done the added task for managing Open Junior High School (SMP Terbuka); 5. Learnt facility, as infrastructure, laboratory, library, classroom, sports, et cetera.

b. Power

Power that needed at Open Junior High School (SMP Terbuka) involved principal, vice, teacher/tutor, administration, and others staff.

c. Student

1. Student that could received at Open Junior High School (SMP Terbuka) were;
    a) Output based level (SD);
    b) School-ages Junior High School (SMP) as the rule;
    c) transfer from others Junior High School (SMP);
    d) Healthy Spirit and Physical;
    e) A good behavior.

2. Totally student that could received at Open Junior High School (SMP Terbuka) must be as much as with able to the management.

3. When received student better noticed its distance where their lived to learnt activity maximal ± 4 km.

d. Curriculum

Thing that needed to design integrated with curriculum were; 1. Prepared based design lerant activity at Open Junior High School (SMP Terbuka); 2. Supplied learnt material that theirs needed; 3. Arrangement lesson schedule and learnt activity where at learnt activity placed; 4. Supplied instrument learnt media that theirs needed; 5. Arrangement schedule through the radio and coorperated with Radio Republic Indonesia.

e. Coorperated Relationship

Coorperated relationship hoped involved were; 1. Region Leader, for founding supported and contributed learnt facility, expert power, and financial; 2. Station broadcasting like Radio Republic Indonesia that have schedule and education programme Open junior High School (SMP Terbuka).

f. Finance; Management and Supplied.

Management Open Junior High School (SMP Terbuka) needed financial operational and investor. This finance from any kind source that relevant with appointment that their haved, were; (a) finance regular, (b) contributed central government, (c) community contributed (BP3), (d) contributed region government, and (e) others source contributed.

Total financial operational Open Junior High School (SMP Terbuka) have appointment, were; 1) Honorarium principal, teacher/tutor and administration; 2) Equipment office; 3) teacher meeting; 4) Learnt tools; 5) Student activity; 6) Commucation and Transportation; 7) Building Maintance, equipment lesson and office.

3. Monitoring Open Junior High School (SMP Terbuka)

To increased effectifity, efficiency, and accomplish the education purposed Open Junior High School (SMP Terbuka), thus used function monitoring against management Open Junior High School (SMP Terbuka) its very important. In education management based school, the good monitoring with principal activities and government office integrated cross sectoral (education

Serviced and Technics Team) at region or from the central must done as formal, informal as with management Open Junior High School (SMP Terbuka), so that policy purpose to accomplish the compulsory education nine years.

In Operasional Pointed Book Open Junior High School (SMP Terbuka). Depdiknas, (2005:66), called that *monitoring* have done with purposed to find data and information from fields tah could used for importance guide. Although the monitoring of Open Junior High School (SMP Terbuka) consist of; (a) central Supervision, were Technics Team Open Junior High School (SMP Terbuka) that consist of unsure Midle and Based Education Management General Directorat and unsure Communication Telecomunication Central, and (b) Region Supervision, were Technics Team or Task Unit from Province Education Serviced.

Target monitoring was Junior High School regular (SMP reguler) and Learnt Activity Placed (LAP). Although that have monitored involve administration and education aspects. Monitoring activity this Open Junior High School (SMP Terbuka) have done good through obesrvation, interview, check list and test.

Principal Open junior High School (SMP Terbuka) as a leader that have given task and responsible against education management at the school of course able to do monitoring and developing potency that theirs. Staff (teacher/tutor and administration) in anticipation each changed, conflict, and decreased or weakness that there are at the school. Beside that result the monitoring as input for management Open Junior High School (SMP Terbuka) as evaluation material rechecked how far education purpose that programme be accomplish. So that the programme policy management Open Junior High School (SMP Terbuka) could repaired and development work School for the future.

4. Programme Evaluation Open Juinor High School (SMP Terbuka)

a). Evaluation Understanding

Evaluation was done considering as the criteria that have agreed and responsibility. Fattah, (2008:107), there are three crucial factors in evaluation concept, were judgement assessment object description, and criteria that defensible criteria. That decision aspect that evaluation different as an activity and from activity other concept, as measurement.

In relationship with education management that evaluation as integrated part from education management, although at micro level (school), meso (Region Education Serviced, Province Education Serviced), or at the macro level (National Educational Department).This thing based by thought that with done evaluation, we could measured advanced level education at the school. Becaused without measured, no reason for saying what the school have advanced or not.

Evaluation about education management at the school, the common have resulted information that could used for taking decision. This Evaluation more focus at programme evaluation, because integrated with crucial leader as policy appoinment.

b). Programme Evaluation Purpose

in education management, programme evaluation purpose Fattah, (2008:108), were; 1) for finding based for lasting consideration a period work, what that have accomplished, what that not yet be accomplished, and what that needed to find a special attention; 2) for guarantee work manner that effective and efficiency that brough organization to use education power source (humankind, infrastructure, financial) as level economics efficiency; 3) to find facta about difficulty, obstacle, deviation have seen from aspect apointed, likes years programme, learnt advanced.

Fattah, (2008:109-110), at commonly programme unsure could appointment with two approached were; (1) Structural approached and (2) Functional approached.

1) Structural approached

Programme unsure a structural approached, were; a) Programme purposed; b) Learnt activity basic selection; c) Rasional and approached against evaluation; and d) Student characteristic (student ability).

2) Functional Approached

Unsure programme as functional approached, were; a) Class climate; b) Administration support system; c) Teacher characteristic; and d) Implelentation style.

Functional approached could considered in all assessment programme at the school. Different with structural approached that main component crucial, but functional approached emphasized at main function from a programme.

In context approached Open Junior High School (SMP Terbuka), where evaluation programme with structural approached focus at unsure programme, were; student component, curriculum, learnt material, learnt activity, infrastructure learnt, power (teacher/tutor and administration), financial and evaluation student. As evaluation programme with functional approached more focus at management Open Junior High School (SMP Terbuka) that have done, were edukative technics activity (study and learning activity), administration technics activity, and reported activity.

Organization institution have a purpose, that must developed with planning that have done with audited (monitoring dan evaluating). All process have audited, were with *monitoring* all activity happened and evaluation as together. This that have to be valuable experienced for the future, could changed will more good than that year before. (Georg S, 1987).

c). Program Evaluation Criteria

There are several criteria that have chosen for using to do evaluation about education programme management that function as study model. Fattah, (2008:112-113), If acuan specific model frame, were economic efficiency evaluation, thus criteria that relevant would chosen for using. But if wide model frame and not definition, was evaluation as much as aspects programme, thus evaluator chosen the most relevant criteria.

Fattah expressed that there are two kind criteria that could used in program evaluation, that's internal and external criterias. Internal criteria was standard that could be applicationed against a programme in programme frame their-self. external criteria was standard that have done against a programme from programme frame out of the source.

1) Internal Criteria.

Internal Criteria; (a) internal criteria that have used, that's coherency.

Coherency was consistency between unsure that unitness, was curriculum evaluation could analysis from; - coherency between evaluation and purpose; -

Coherency between learning activity and purposed; - Coherency evaluation and learning activity; - Coherency between the contain of lesson and purposed; (b) internal criteria that have used, that's source spreaded. What humankind sources that ready and potency that have spesification in programme. Many programme ath the school was failness not because design that not right, but not right chosen the management. In group teaching example: who that chosen as the leader. If the leader that have chosen but could not cooperated orientation, thus group management to accomplish the agreement all team could not effective; (c) used considering, attitude and the useful reaction that participant in programme sometimes to be criteria. From the useful could be criteria, example; satisfied, goal preparation, interest; (d) prepared performance, example; towards performance that prepared the programme, have value with criteria that describe from programme goals that would stand; (e) cost effectiveness, were; quantification cost programme and benefits. But, not necessary the cash money. In analysis cost efectiveness, expressed means result fact that different from money value. Effectiveness money value from finance that involved with programme. Education programme, commonly cost with expensed for personil, facility, material, equipment and subcategori from each categori; (f) Generative ability, was programme ability brought positive results that never accounted before. example, idea results that proved more benefit than goals that expressed at all programme; (g) Impact, that's more effect compared with that may be happened natural, without the programme. As assess impact indicator programme was identification reflect the result.

2) External Criteria

External Criteria; (a) policy towards, usually programme that must done in frame policy appointed. Example; seminar and locacarya, how far programme seminar and locacarya that loyal at the policy that have appointed by project leader; (b) cost Benefit Analysis, that's wanted about a good programme benefit that as soon as appear or that not appear, and programme management cost, although direct cost or indirect cost. Standard indicator monetary unit. Benefit was outcome unit that have found from the programme that maybe consist of from increased community responsible, or increased productivity. Programme cost, that's sources that needed for programme management example; salary, material, traveled cost. Benefit and cost could compared with account one of the below; - benefit cost ratio that's benefit divided cost; - net benefit; benefit minus cost;- internal rate of return; that's benefit that result invest unit; (c) Multiple Effects means that effect multiple as impact at goal group. Usually programme have more from a goal group. Although that means have a goal group, that programme have resulted effect for other goal group. Example environmental education programme student group purpose, but other group as not direct have influenced; parent, brother and sister of student, community at the palced. This impact involved multiple effect programme. Because that sometimes as evaluation have designed for trying expressed multiple effect that the means.

That the learnt as process that internal for each individual, that as result transformation stimulus that from external event around individual that with theirs. So the external condition more used, better organization as at the learnt event. (Miarso, 2007).

d). Evaluation Principle

Evaluation principle that have done as the next; 1) Sustainable principle, means evaluation done as sustain; 2) Total principle, means all aspect in programme (component) evaluation; 3) Principle objektive, means evaluation have deliverance level from subjectivity or evaluator individual drifted off; 4) Principle valid and credentials, that's have internal consistency and measured what must be measured; 5) Principle criteria using, that's criteria internal and external for evaluation programme, and for evaluation learnt result, usually used criteria standard ultimate and norma criteria (standard relative); 6) Principle useful, meants evaluation that have done so to be used, although for the leader, or staff.

From describe about criteria programme evaluation above, could said that for assessment a programme that have done advance or not, sure necessary a criteria and how far impact management although that positive or negative for programme management school and community.

In relation with management Open Junior High School (SMP Terbuka), thus criteria evaluation programme that have used was pointed a target that to be accomplished or the purpose of Open Junior High School (SMP Terbuka). As have described at the discussion before that purpose Open Junior High School (SMP Terbuka) at the basic was for receiving output Junior (SD) that because geography condition and obstacle economy social to continue their education to level Junior High School (SMP), and one supported design the compulsory education Junior (Dikdas) nine years. (Depdiknas, 2005:7). With there are Open Junior High School (SMP Terbuka) be hoped could supported or be accomplished Governmant Policy (Depdiknas) about nine years compulsory education at the region.

Education system very needed motoring and evaluation so that reflect how far development oe advanced from the education result. With evaluation, thus forwards and backwards quality education could know. With evaluation too, we could know weakness point and easy seek out to change to be better for the future.

Function and purpose evaluation were; 1. To know advanced the student after learnt one or two semester; 2. To know efficiency level education method that used one or two semester.

From evaluation result management schoola principal, teacher/tutor and administration could make a new paradigm, make changing at external and internal condition that sustainable. So condemnation condition organization to be flexibel and efective. (Peter, 1956).

Teacher/tutor as the first step, their received all the material and training from education system to teach that efective, so that not invented student difficulty. This effectiveness that are done everyday, for provisioning against national examination that the future. With good and regular education planning, thus the result would satisfy. (Stuart, 2008)

Means satisfy serviced, were relation a good principal, teacher/tutor and administration with ability each staff. Organization the institution process with quqlity, thus stakeholder that have chosen the institution would be satisfied. (Nazir, 2002).

CHAPTER II
Research Method

This chapter describe about: a. Research Planning and Approached; b. Research Location; c. Source Data; d. Technical Collected Data; e. Technical Analysis Data; f. Recheck Valid Data; g. Research Steps.

This things as continue describe research planning and approached, research location, source data, technical collected data, technical analysis data, and recheck valid data.

A. Research Planned and Approached

1. Research Approch

This research used quality approached. Quality research approached by Bogdan dan Biklen (1998) said; quality research was; observation the person at environmental life, effort to know its language and its around.

Management open Junior High School was institution education, that given opportunity to student finish its education. To know what phenomenon about it. What unknown and bersifat inductive character in concept development at the data.

Patton, (1980:5), quality method as special have many data that many cases about many people. Quality data prepared very specify through expression as direct and description that accurate programme, event, interaction and behavior that observer.

2. Research Planning

This research have done at three sites that different, were; Open Junior High School (SMP Terbuka) Teratai, Open Junior High School (SMP Terbuka) Tulip and Open Junior High School (SMP Terbuka) Mawar. This research planning were multi-sites, be hoped could used in development theory. Because research have done a site that the sites more than one site. This things as an earned of Bogdan and Biklen (1998;2) said;

> When researchers study two or more subjects, or depositories of data they are usually doing what we call multisite studies. Multisite studies take a variety of forms. Some start as a single site only to leave the original work serve as the first in series of studies or as the pilot for a multisite study other studies are primarily single siie studies but indude less intense, less extensive observation at other sites for the purpose of addressing the question of general izability. Other researches do comparative site studies are done and then compared and contasted.

From the expression could known that characteristic main multi-sites were if research two or more subject research, or place for saving data with as compare each site. Research planning study this multi-sites given more that research would had a good experience, a good experience thought as theoretical although skill in collected data have done with difficult, and type of planning were approached "*constant comparative method..*" Data would be collected and analysis for developing model descriptive that cover at all phenomenon sites. In *constant comparative method,* that the steps have done at this research were as the next; (1) collected data at the first site, was Open Junior High School (SMP Terbuka) Teratai. Research have done till at the level satisfied data, and that during have done categorization in themes for invented change process at the school; (2) Done observed at second site, was Open Junior High School (SMP Terbuka) Tulip. This observer aim to find inventing that integrated with management principal in changed process; (3) research be continue at site the third Open Junior High School (SMP Terbuka) Mawar, with aim that same. Although collected data in this research be done as a step, although in a special events, observed have done as simultaneous, an instance at managed school programme, activity and certainly event that needed special time. In this things research advantage the *event* for digging data.

B. Research Area

This research have done with taken location at Open Junior High School (SMP Terbuka) 01, 02, 05 at Malang region. This location research have chosen with *purposive* from the fifth Open Junior High School (SMP Terbuka) 01, 02, 03, 04 and 05 with that different location because have several unique as the next;

1. SMP Terbuka 01 at SMP Neg. 02 (SMP Terbuka Teratai) District Klojen-Malang at district central business and between two market (big market and comboran market).

SMP Terbuka 02 at SMP Neg. 16 (SMP Terbuka Tulip) District Blimbing-Malang near terminal and between two resident (Araya resident and Teluk resident). SMP Terbuka 05 at SMP Neg. 18 (SMP Terbuka Mawar) District Lowokwaru-Malang resident region Geria Santa though at central crowd, activity learning relative did not disturbed because wide area about SMP Negeri ± 10.100 m² as center school, this community environment was community educational/International Education City. (Statistik Indonesia, 2003).

2. Student purpose this Open Junior High School (SMP Terbuka) was serviced students output SD/MI especially that 13-15 years or maximal 18 years that unadvantge because economy social condition, limitness transportation facility, geography condition that impossible they are followed the lesson as usual at Junior High School (SMP) reguler.

3. Education system concept that have used at Open junior High School (SMP Terbuka) was open education system or far distance study system with used modul as self study source for the student. Learning system through tutorial serviced that managed at Junior High School Regular (SMP regular) with guided by the teacher/tutor, and learning serviced at the Learnt Activity Placed (LAP).

4. Teached and learnt activity the Open Junior High School (SMP Terbuka) more focused at student-self learnt activity with modul at LAP. Total LAP Open Junior High School (SMP Terbuka) were three (3) LAP where spread far at the village that distance far each others.

Tabel 2.1. DATA CONDITION LIST STUDENT Open Junior High school (SMP Terbuka) 01 Malang.

No	Name / LAP	Condition Student										
		Class 1			Class 2			Class 3			Total	
		M	F	T	M	F	T	M	F	T	M	F
1	TKB Pelita 1 /A	19	21	40	10	21	31	18	18	36	47	60
2	TKB Pelita 2 /B	20	19	39	12	19	31	19	14	33	51	52
3	TKB Pelita 3/C	22	13	35	15	15	30	-	-	-	37	28
	Jumlah	**61**	**53**	**114**	**37**	**55**	**92**	**37**	**32**	**69**	**135**	**140**

NAME/ ADDRESS, TOTAL STUDENT PER LAP SMP T. T

No	Nama /tempat TKB	Alamat	Jumlah siswa			
			Kelas 1	Kelas 2	Kelas 3	Jumlah
1	TKB Pelita 1/A	Jl Moh Yamin 60	40	31	36	107
2	TKB Pelita 2/B	Jl Moh Yamin 60	39	31	33	103
3	TKB Pelita 3/C	Jl Moh Yamin 60	35	30		65
	Jumlah		114	92	69	275

Tabel 2.2. Identification at SMP Terbuka 01 Malang Tahun 2009/2010

No.	Profession	Ijazah terakhir yang Dimiliki								
		SD	SMP	SMA	PGSLP/ D1	D2/A2	SM/D3/ A3	S1	S2	Jml
1.	Principal	-	-	-	-	-	-	-	1	1
2.	Vice	-	-	-	-	-	-	1	-	1
3.	Teacher	-	-	-	-	2	5	17	-	24
4.	Tutor	-	-	-	-	-	2	2	-	4
5.	Staff	-	-	2	-	-	-	-	-	2
6.	Office boy	-	1	-	-	-	-	-	-	1
	Total	-	1	2	-	2	7	20	1	33

Tabel 2.3. Total Student SMP Terbuka 02 Malang tahun pelajaran 2009/2010

No	Name LAP	Siswa Kelas VII			Siswa Kelas VIII			Siswa Kelas 3			Jumlah		
		L	P	Jml	L	P	Jml	L	P	Jml	L	P	Jml
1	Raden Intan	23	19	42	27	21	47	13	12	25	**63**	**52**	**115**

Tabel 2.4. Identification at SMP Terbuka 02 Malang Tahun 2009/2010

No.	Profession	Ijazah terakhir yang Dimiliki								
		SD	SMP	SMA	PGSLP/D1	D2/A2	SM/D3/A3	S1	S2	Jml
1.	Principal	-	-	-	-	-	-	-	1	1
2.	Vice	-	-	-	-	-	-	1	-	1
3.	Teacher	-	-	-	-	2	-	17	-	19
4.	Tutor	-	-	-	-	-	-	4	-	4
5.	Staff	-	1	2	-	-	-	-	-	3
6.	Office boy	2	-	-	-	-	-	-	-	2
	Total	**2**	**1**	**2**	**-**	**2**	**-**	**22**	**1**	**30**

Tabel 2.5. Total Student SMP Terbuka 05 Malang tahun 2009/2010

No	Name LAP	Class I			Class II			Class III			Total		
		M	F	T	M	F	T	M	F	T	M	F	T
1	Soekarno Hatta 1	34	11	45	19	25	44	14	15	29	57	61	118
2	Soekarno Hatta 2												
3	Al Kaaf				7		7	7	1	8	14	1	15
	Jumlah	16	25	41	21	22	43	14	14	28	71	62	133

Noted: That follow skill programme class I and II Total participant 30 student with male = 20 student and Famale = 10 student

Tabel 2.6. Powerness at SMP Terbuka 05 Malang

No.	Profession	Last Certificate that their had							
		SMP	SMA	D1	D2/A2	SM/D3/A3	SAR-JANA	S2	Total
1.	Principal	-	-	-	-	-	-	1	1
2.	Vice	-	-	-	-	-	1	-	1
3.	Teacher	-	-	-	-	-	24	-	24
4.	Tutor	-	-	-	-	-	9		9
5.	Staff	-	1	-	-	-	3		4
6	Office boy	1	-	-	-	-	-	-	1
	Total	1	1	-	-	-	37	1	40

Mayority student lived around the school that spread at three district were SMP Terbuka 01 Kecamatan Klojen, SMP Terbuka 02 Kecamatan Blimbing, SMP Terbuka 05 Kecamatan Lowokwaru, so would be integrated custom and traditions between district. Their from family that never till at the midle education, at the midle till below economy, and their parent'job heterogen. All unsure of the school foremost advanced at the technology and science.

Potency of Junior High School (SMP) State Malang as the mother could enpower and use to support fluently learning at the Open junior High School (SMP Terbuka) Malang, especially teacher/tutor, infrastructure. For the future very be hoped Open Junior High School (SMP Terbuka) Malang could increase the education quality and parallel with Junior High School (SMP) other State, the things very enabled.

Basic study documentation integrated with special education build management for Junior and High education (SD and SMP) at Malang region, where this management education have reached the far district with able to increase poverty population access against education.

For building management Junior and High education (SD and SMP) year 2007/2008 at Malang region, from study documentation could image commonly as the next;

1. Government Malang region, (2009) expressed; extension Malang district 110.06 km² with total population 836.131 soul, that spread at five (5) district. Each district were; Klojen district = 134.779 soul, Blimbing district = 174.521 soul, Kedungkandang district = 170.647 soul, Sukun district = 184.755 soul, Lowokwaru district = 171.429 soul), 57 village-head. From amount this village, that involved categori far village were 10 villages 505 RW and 3.649 RT. (Statistik Indonesia, 2003).

2. Total population study-ages 8-12 years Junior (SD) was 7.287 person. Population study-ages 13-15 years Junior High School (SMP) was 3.622 person.

3. Total Junior High School (SMP) as much as 5 Junior High School (SMP), with total student all ages 13-15 years was 1.449 student. Total new student (class VII) was 553 student.

4. Integrated with Work Participant Point (WPP) and Participant Point (APP), that's for (WPP) SD/MI = 108.91%, and (APP) SD/MI = 93.87%. (WPP) SMP/MTs = 70,96%, an (APP) SMP/MTs = 56,46%. Rasio student per class for Junior (SD/MI) was 28 student, and for Junior High School (SMP/MTs) was 51 student. (Government Malang region, 2009).

Obviously from prefigured education building management special Junior education at Malang region integrated information and data Open Junior High School (SMP Terbuka) included that there are at Malang region at the fact not yet have documentation "Profile education at Malang region 2009/2010 year". So that have found information and data that enough comprehensive about Open Junior High School (SMP Terbuka) especislly at Malang region, thus to know and don analysis integrated nine years compulsory education through education serviced model Open Junior High School (SMP Terbuka) needed to do field study.

From the back ground problem about Junior education management above,specially integrated with implementation policy nine years compulsory education programme Open Junior High School (SMP Terbuka), thus the writer interested for doing research to use concepts management Open Junior High School (SMP Terbuka) field. Subject research means was "Management Open Junior High School (SMP Terbuka) in nine years compulsory education (Study Multi-Sites at three Open Junior High School (SMP Terbuka) Teratai, Tulip, Mawar, at Malang region)." Management nine years compulsory education programme that have done at Open Junior High School Regular (SMP regular) as managed at the district. Operational management Open junior High School (SMP Terbuka) have vision, mision and purpose that parallel with national education purpose, and done management that integrated with components school, were; (1) student, (2) curriculum, (3) learnt material, (4) Learnt activity, (5) instrument, (6) teacher/tutor, and (7) learnt evaluation. Management contained power source rule that effective and efficiency with function and responsible management. Function management that have done study in this research, there are four basics components as the next; 1. Planning; 2. Organization; 3. Development; 4. Audit. The four component as cycle process that called PODA. The four management function as basic function that always there are.

1. Planning management Open Junior High School (SMP Terbuka) was in nine years compulsory education programme at Malang region; a. attitude managed management and created relationship that balanced and not discriminative, given serviced that fast, made easy and efforted to satisfy with that have done basic rational constant. Principal enjoy the job that substance its character not as formality, and done as ready and carefully; b. principal liked direct work to visit management clss and not only at the table, enjoy walked to control the class, say hello direct to the teacher/tutor and student, always given wayout to teacher/tutor with easy, principal liked to call and given direct towards to vice, teacher/tutor and student, done a new one and maneuver, unliked to drag the job, and put with all soul for school; c. motivation and put principle *"the big dreams"* as the door result to manage the school, could work different with others, creative and initiative, always towards at the school vision, mision and worked with carefully not with rasio.

2. Organizasian management Open Junior High School (SMP Terbuka) was in nine years compulsory education programme at Malang region; a. principal made *job description* between vice, teacher/tutor and others worked team as proportional and professional, divided all the responsibility, and functional each job at the school; b. always done their job with full awared at the school vision and mission, only without sanction and principal undiscipline, always made their-self right, and their job given only to the believer person; c. principal have divided task and respomsibility to the teacher/tutor, have done their job, task and each function as the rule, created relationship that not *"overlapping."* And made internal coordination meeting and period or tentative teacher/tutor meeting; d. principal towards a good cooperated and with the teacher/tutor. Made the policy school with all the teacher/tutor idea, and all activities as family.

3. Development management power source Open Junior High School (SMP Terbuka) **w**as nine years compulsory education at Malang region; a. as quantity, still less teracher/tutor for any lesson, since empowered honorarium teacher/tutor. As quality, teacher/tutor still not yet passed certification, not yet graduate (S1), many teacher not professional. So that many teacher/tutor could not teach; b. as quantity, have completed physic facility, instruments, a comfortable classroom, multimedia room, principal and vice rooms, sciences laboratorium, library, learnt media, infrastructure sports. Ready for use and good condition, only it used not optimal and maintance; c. as with the routine budget, financial central Government or region, and from *"generating income."* As finance quality and cost still good enough because undiscipline managed the *"cash flow"* since consequences unhealthy.

4. Managemnt audit sistem Open Junior High School (SMP Terbuka) at the nine years compulsory education programme at Malang region; a. The expert principal, used

systematic language, distrinct intonation, with convinced language, supporting direct source and original, experience, religious, discerment; b. message that called as soon as, from the true fact, accurately, called as scholl vision and mission; c. supporting media with many alternative media that school'had and prepared, easy to find fairness media, with reprentative media; d. could receive the good message. Education management alternative with Open Junior High School (SMP Terbuka) level that managed at Junior High School regular (SMP regular), that needed their student learnt their-self with limited guided from other person. (Depdiknas, 2005:5).

C. Data Source

In qualitative research the informan as a source that could give information. Data source as a crucial process of this research, because only with found accurately data thus process research would finish to find its answer from the research have their focused. Data that wanted to collect, was information that as the research purposed. Although data source that have used in this research were; all of principal, teacher/tutor, ministration and student as informan.

Informan have chosen as purposive. This things mean for choosing the right informan relevant and competence with research problem so that data could use. And key informan from the others that could give information, and et cetera.

Criteria informan in this research, were (1) still active as the teacher/tutor at the school; (2) intensive in an institution activity at the organization school; (3) informan still have time to give information to researcher.

Data source have found through *"purposive snowball sampling."* In this research, that as informan was a head of the nine years compulsory education programme at office national education (Diknas) at Malang region, and principal Junior High School regular (SMP regular) and/or Open Junior High School (SMP Terbuka) at Malang. That informan were; vice, teacher/tutor, StafF ministration and commiteee/board school Open Junior High School (SMP Terbuka) at Malang region.

In this research used to net information from a head of the nine years compulsory education programme at the office national education (Diknas) at Malang region, Principal, vice, teacher/tutor, staff ministration and committee/board school Open Junior High School (SMP Terbuka) at Malang region with task and competency as much as 32 person. Material or information that netting through the document as with research purpose, tha's management nine years compulsory education programme Open Junior High School (SMP Terbuka) at Malang region, monitoring and evaluation that supported and obstacled implementation the compulsory education programme, and policy contribution level programme that have done against increased participation point school at Malang region. So that build actual profile, the reality learnt management that as empiric reconstruction result. Process learnt management that as process audit, with this research got three (3) actual profile from each Open Junior High School (SMP Terbuka) about learning. At analysis, have done integrated so that come at the actually profile.

D. Data Collected Technical

With data source, thus technic that used for collecting data in this research were; (1) indepth interviewing about data that relationship with focus first and second, even bewared the original data level have done also interview with teacher/tutor that especial different good in the teacher/tutor'room. Indepth interviewing have done minimal once each theirs, but this research each data that have done two-three times especially the crucial data by research; (2) participant observation so that data always the righteousness; and (3) study document with integrated prob;em management increased teacher competency at the school as conscientious (Bogdan & Biklen, 1998; Sonhaji, 1994).

Event, that's any event or social situation with result indepth interviewing, participant observation and integrated with problem and research focus. Events that observation integrated with educative technics activity (learnt activity) and ministration technics activity at Open Junior High School (SMP Terbuka) at Malang region. Process to each Open Junior High School (SMP Terbuka) Three times, and principal met their staff, teacher/tutor that have any time to give input. That their met and asked as the focus, as compared and rechecked the information reliable value. Study document that relevant with problem and research focus, like curriculum, learnt material, statistic output and drop out, learnt schedule, learnt task, student study result, student and teacher/tutor present list, school map and school infrastructure that have prepared at research location.

Data that have collected that reflected comparing between reality learnt management that collected through; informan, indepth interviewing, participant observation, and study document.

Indepth interviewing, participant observation was formed comunication between two person, a person wanted to find information from the others with any questions based the purposed. Indepth interviewing, and participant observation as a big line divided two, were participant observation unstructure and participant observation have structure. indepth interviewing, unstructure sometimes also called intensive indepth interviewing. And indepth interviewing have structure sometimes also called standardized interview, that the question have written with question chosen that have prepared. (Mulyana, 2008:180).

participant observation that have done research in this research was participant observation. Mean in data collexted or information that integrated with the events or activity management

Open Junior High School (SMP Terbuka) at the research location, the research have ability, skill observation, assessment, accurated against research environmental, and ability in bewared any obstacle that maybe happened (involved difficult adaptation and comunication with community that was be researched), and with disertai kemampuan imagination ability that strong to formulate research result. Mulyana, (2008:176) said that observation as potential to find a perfect data, example about social event, the former event and followed, and expressed the mean by the participant and the witness persons for eternal, an after the event done. For fluently the observation in this research thus needed to prepare about events that to be research focus with technic used observation sheet.

Study document was data collected instrument, and the data source as the noted or study document that have prepared, beside that also called as secondary source. Faisal, (2005:53). Therefore, for fluently noted data or information that needed as with research purposed, thus arranged the research dan prepared format documentation or sheet study document. Faisal, (2005:137) expressed with there are the form study document that have prepared, research only noted the data that needed at the form that have arranged and prepared by research, with noted document could more systematic and to be focused (selective).

Sutopo, (2003:124) expressed that study document and file as data source tahat during have crucial position in qualitative research. Especially if styudy target towards at back ground or any event that happened before that very integrated with condition or event thus now in research.

E. Data Analysis Technical

In qualitative research or naturalistic research, what data their found at the research? But as interaction research between the researcher and data source. Interaction involved given interpretation research against what that have given or said by informan. Therefore, data analysis technic in this research at the basic have begun with collected data, till finished this research.

Data analysis technic during collected data as the begining analysis against data that have found. The analysis could efforted wuth what that called activity data reduction. Reduction data could mean as process chosen and research attention central through selection that fast against focus that could be study, a sharpened focus, made data collected summary result, organization data so ready to analysis after have done as whole collected data.

Last analysis purpose or the data reduction activity for knowing the whole data that have collected and data not yet netting. Besides that through the data reduction activity could think the next collected data that the quality sometimes more good for containing the less data or ideas that appeared during collected data.

Data analysis technic in this research was induktive-conseptualistic technic means information empiris that have found and build concepts or proporsition towards development a substantive theory. Becaused this research design used study multi-sites, noted this study document, by Yin, (1984) called as *"content analysis"*, and that means research analysis data have done two steps were; (a) analysis data individual cases; and (b) analysis data cross-cases analyzis.

(1). Analysis data individual sites.

Analysis data site individual cases that means in this research, was data from each subject. Analysis data step that have done together with collected data and to follow the pointed of, Bogdan and Biklen, (1998), involved; (1) research focus constant, what constant as the design, pr needed to change; (2) arranged invented for a while as the data where have collected; (3) the designer with the next collecting data only the invented collecting data before; (4) analytic questions develop in frame the next collecting data; (5) suggestion collected data (informan, situation, document).

The fifth activities could do as integrated through the next steps;

First, each moment and finished for at once collected data and made research memo, a reflection against process and collected data result that is doing. Research memo contained a while invented, ideas that appear, and design the next collected data.

Second, after finishing to do several time collected data, all noted field have read, known and made the summary. (Miles dan Huberman, 1992) the summary called contact summary. Contact summary was the sheet that contained a short result describe against of all the field noted, focused, and solution against problem formulated.

Third, every three weeks or a mount, all contact summary that have finished and read oncemore. Miles and Huberman, (1992) than made site summary. Site summary was a while result summary that included what have known about site and pointed what that still must netted for the next. Done with analysis involved; (1) develop system code categori; (2) sorted data, and (3) give the conclusion.

In development system code categori, all data that noted from field, included contact summary and site summary while never have made during read collected data and rechecked with carefully. After rechecking the identification topic and made group in its categories. Each topic categori have made code that imaged include the topic purpose. The code have to be instrument to organizer units data. So the code could have function as there are, thus to each code hae given limited operational as included the purposed.

Sortir data have done after code category system. All code and limited operational have made, all field noted read again, and each unit data that there are have given the same code. This unit data was a field noted that usually as sentence, an alinea, or several alinea. The codes have written at the edge sheet field noted. Then all the units data have sorted or made its groups.

Study data was a group information that arrange as systematic that given there are made the conclusion. With other word, study data as a process arranged information as systematic to find invented research conclusion. Study data have done as systematic and the clear lines, so that easy followed by reader. Besides it, analysis data also could do since beginning and as a long research process. Research could use analysis data according Miles dan Huberman, (1992:15-20) with procedure "reduction data, study data, and have conclusion/verification" as the next;

a) Study Data

Study data or *display data* means made easy for research to see the whole imaged or parts of the research. Therefore this research, research would study data in the form matrics, grafic, *network* and *charts*.

b) Reduction Data

Data that have found at the research location (field data) put in describe or complete report and details. Fields report by research needed reduction, made summary, chosen at the subject things, focused at the subject things, then made seek the theme or design. Reduction data used during the research process. During collected data with reduction data, summary, code, check the theme, made ideas, and written memo.

c) Have Conclusion

Verification data at this qualitative research have done as long as research process. Since begun to come at the field and during research collected data process effoted to analysis and seek the purposed from collected data were; seek design, theme, equal relation, things that sometimes appeared, and as that put at the conclusion that have tentative, with added data through process verification thus have conclusion that have *grounded*. Others word each conclusion always done verification during at the research. The components analysis data, called as "comparative model", could image as the next;

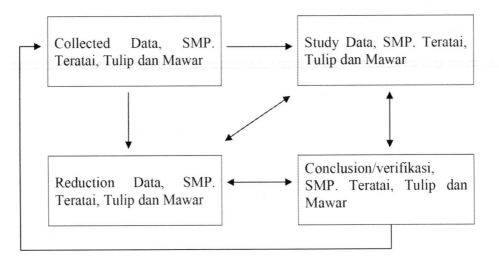

Figure 2.1 Data Analysis Interactive Model. (Miles dan Huberman, 1992).

(2) Trans-sites Analysis Data

Cross-sites analysis data that means as process to compare the invented that have done each site, at once as the process involved between site. Proportion and this substantive theory and analysis with compared proportion and substance theory from invent site, used for seeking unique and different characteristic from each site as concept theory different basic. This different sites have to be while invented to use confirmation with the next sites. Simulant analysis have done with interconnected between proportion and subtansive theory at sites to reconstruction, concept arranged about equaly sites as systematic.

Have done analysis cross sites with the same technic that have done at the sites. Analysis that last in this cross site means to arrange concept systimatic at the data analysis result and interpretation theory that as proportion narative cross site that to be material to develop substance theory. Analysis made to describe towards to describe phenomenon that means integrated causal about the phenomenon.

Design that's approached "*constant comparative method..*" Data have collected and analysis to development descriptive model that involved all sites phenomenon. In *constant comparative method,* although have done all the steps in this research were as the next; (1) Done to collect data at the first site, that's Open Junior High School (SMP Terbuka) Teratai. Research done till at level satisfiedness data, and during that have done categorization in the theme to invent changing process at the school; (2) Done observation at second site, that's Open Junior High School (SMP Terbuka) Tulip. This observer purposed to find invented that integrated with management principal in changed process; (3) research at third site Open Junior High School (SMP Terbuka)

48

Mawar, with the same purposed. Although collected data in thid research have done step by step, in a special events, observer done with simulant, example at school management programme, activity and event that needed special time. In this things research used the *event* to dig the data.

F. Data Valid Recheck,

This research so to be valid, thus needed to recheck the valid data. In qualitative research, research as the main informan. Therefore, validity test and reliability instrument not with testing the instrument, but through credibility recheck and audit the data. Lincoln dan Guba (1985). Purposed have done credibility test was proved so far the research data contained the truth so that could be believed.

Data valid recheck that used in this research at third criteria basic, were; (1) credibility; (2) dependability; (3) confirmability.

1. Credibility

Understanding the credibility data needed to do for proving the events that observer by the research true have done with what that real happened atb the field. Credential value data in qualitative reserach used to make criteria/value truth that have *emic*, good for reader or subjekct that research.

Creswell (2005) recomendation used multi strategy rechecked accurate invent. There are eight strategy to find accurated data that proposed, were; (1) data source triangulation; (2) rechecked the member; (3) used many description for watching the invented; (4) clarification research as informan; (5) study negative information or in contrast with the theme; (6) taken many time at the research location; (7) discuss with peer made a high accurate invent; and (8) used expert auditor review the all invented.

In this research rechecked credibility data according Lincoln and Guba, (1985) that involved; (1) observation that done as persistent observation; (2) data source triangulation; (3) *member check*; (4) peer reviewing; and (5) referential adequacy checks.

First, rechecked credential value data in this research that have done persistent observation with continue research integrated at the field with means to supply data that much necessary. Taken more time to collect data in this research means to extend the scope and build relationship believed to each other with informan so that more opened to give information. Observer sustainable means to find data that happened as consisten/designer so that avoid from invented only a moment or that suddenly appeared. With this technic hoped would to separate the urgent aspect, and not urgent so could do a centre noticed at the aspect that relevant with research focus.

The second done triangulation Lincoln and Guba, (1985) there are four models were; data source triangulation, research triangulation, theory triangulation and method triangulation. In this research used two methods were; data source triangulation and method triangulation.

Method triangulation done as used several method that different to check again credibility data or information that have found, example; resuly interview about time skill practical have compared with practical activity observation, then check again with document that relevant were practical activity jurnal and student present list. If happened different information, thus chosen information that have found from two data collected method and research perception with noticed source triangulation result.

The third, data check with member check done with subject interview through two manner. The first manner when interviewing in form message idea that caught by researcher when interview. The second manner as indirect in form message summary interview and field noted that have made by research to essence informan, to comment, decreased or increased that necessary. Commentary, reaction, added or minus used to revision field noted.

The fourth, discuss peer reviewing would do with manner discussion data that have collected with peer reviewing that have expert that relevant.

The fifth, recheck about referential adequacy checks means to correct equipment data with seen again the original data. Each interview efforted used tapecorder, and when observation used camera. Transcrip from tapecorder and photo rechecked with accurately. Referential adequacy checks in this research done with rechecked report manuscript with data original at the filed.

2. Dependability

Dependability done to assess process that have done during the research, that as research result report. For that needed dependent auditor. As dependent auditor in this research were; the third our promotor.

Process checked auditor basic data and report that have given by research. The steps of research, research made report with data that needed to auditor. Auditor as separated discuss with research the noted of data and report. Input from auditor used to repaire report manuscript. After repaired, the manuscript that given back to auditor for the last rechecking and agreeing for the report.

3. Comfirmability

Comfirmability needed to know objectiveness data that found, objektive or not. This things hoped at the several person as an agreement, view, idea, and invent. If several person or all of have objective agreement, however emphasized only at the data. For the assure data in this research have done with comfirmation data with all informan or all the expert. This activity done together with the dependability audit.

G. Research Steps

Bogdan & Biklen, (1998) said; that qualitative research steps involved; (1) pre-field activity, (2) field activity, and (3) intensive analysis. Creswell, (2005) proposed qualitative research steps were; (1) identify intent and accres-type design, and relate intent to your research problem; (2) discuss approval and acces considerations; (3) use appropriate data collection procedures; (4) analyze and interpret data within a design; and (5) write the report consisten with your design.

As big line of this research process management have done three steps, were; prepared step, research managed step, and research reported step.

The first, prepared step. Were; (1) seek issue that interest in context education management, (2) study a lot of literature that relevant with management Open Junior High School (SMP Terbuka), (3) made the study focus at the education management Open Junior High School (SMP Terbuka), (4) made orientation study at the subject that wanted be research, for the three Open Junior High School (SMP Terbuka) at Malang region.

The second, research managed step divided two were; common exploration and focus explorastion. Common exploration involved activity; (1) consultation, interview and permission to the institutions; (2) common watched at the object that have done observation and interview as global.

Common invented basic then exploration at each site focus, involved; (1) collected data have done as detail to invent the theme conceptual frame at the field; (2) collected data each site and single analysis data, continue analisis data together between site; (3) result checked and research invent by auditor.

The third, research report writer. In this report writer step, have several stepe that must be noticed by the research. Lincoln & Guba, (1985) there are three task, were; a. arranged index material data so have taken again as fast if their needed; b. Made outline, while report. This outline prepared in frame work; c. Made cross-reference at the material that have given index while outline.

CHAPTER III

Research Invented And Flattened Data

This chaptes described about: (a) research flattened data, (b) research data analysis, and (c) research invented. Research data flattened consist of three sites were: flattened data site I; SMP Terbuka 01 (Teratai) Malang, flattened data site II; SMP Terbuka 02 (Tulip) Malang, flattened data site III; SMP Terbuka 05 (Mawar) Malang, and analysis trans-case. Research invented consist of: research invented at site I; SMP Terbuka 01 (Teratai) Malang, Research invented consist of: research invented at site II; SMP Terbuka 02 (Tulip) Malang, Research invented consist of: research invented at site III; SMP Terbuka 05 (Mawar) Malang, and research invented trans-site.

A. Research Flattened Data

1. Flattened Data Site I at Open Junior High School Teratai at Malang Region.

a. School Planned about Management Site I at Open Junior High School Teratai Malang Region.

See from management planning attitude factor have efficiency represntative was not attitude individual but there are "manager attitude," and simple organization structure relationship, not a special acceptance "gold-child" all of same important for the school, principal liked more-fast, more-good and if could fast and easy why must late and difficult, so its impact and serviced at the school "when and where was happened" proved when we are walking around the school for rechecking the classroom at the field-sport there is a teacher need sign of the principal and as son as he signs the letter.

Principal known about its task and function as a leader and management as contextual, proved with result what that he have said as the next.

Remember, as principal not only at our job room, but any where, when must as a good principal, not arrogant. Not only by four walls building room'principal, but "many limits" must known that rule …. Do not talk only without work. This life must always changed each time, same with school as my life, and the most effective changed by our teachers and if we must "jumped" that able changed, but as a certainty that have done, with little laugh like did not wanted like that (F1/A/SMPT/150710/13.00-15.00 wita).

A teacher have said when rested and result the speaked as the next.

Principal was not arrogant only our impression, very "*fair*" and known to each others. This school have been his life, happy. Principal very noticed that the creative teacher/tutor, wanted to work hard, and have ability in their sciences, and the vice have chosen was the correct person, as a conceptor and happy with theirs job, the impact all of the teacher/tutor respected, with smile (F1/A/SMPT/150710/13.00-15.00 wita).

Principal of this school planned, vice, and all the staff, teacher/tutor involved have managerial done learning at the school. They always with regulation school that known with their discipline, they respected to each others, but have towards freely, and as common principal and each teacher/tutor have known what must theirs job, with always wanted more good and professional. For obviously could see the next table.

Tabel 3.1. School Planned about Management Site I at Open Junior High School (SMP Terbuka) Teratai at Malang Region.

Factor ann Dimention	Quality
1. Attitude Management	
a. What that must done	Managerial attitude, created relationship that balanced and
	not descriminative, given a good serviced, easily, and efforted to satisfy but always rational as the rule was done, principal enjoyed his job that was substance not as formality, and done with enjoy and carefully.
b. Ability to managed	Principal enjoyed to come each classes and not only at the

	table, walking to control all the class, say hello to the teacher/tutor and student direct, always given way out to the teacher/tutor, principal always called and given direct towards to the vice, teacher/tutor and student, made maneuver, never kept the job for the future, and done with all soul to school.
c. Motivation and desired	Put principle "*the big dreams*" as the door of succeed management school, bear done different with the others, creative and initiative, always done at the school vision, mission and worked with carefully not with ratio.

b. Organization Management Open Junior High School (SMP Terbuka) Teratai at Malang Region.

Seen from this school organizaation structure factor have done enough good, responsible coordination of the principal to the vice, staff, and teacher/tutor about the "*job description*" each person have known their job and what that must done. Principal done "*to manage*" and given towards and always checked and evaluation all their responsibility, likes as coordinator that responsible to all management mechanism at the school. Responsibilty that have given to their with management operational standard or policy of the school. So that management and responsible could walk with good and optimal, principal have given all. When principal have spoken all of in the meeting room, have taken several commitment that could done as idea reference as the next.

The wickness of principal, and the leader commonly at the institution especially their "heart," means that honest given trust as optimal? If not yet able liked that thus did not be a leader and did not managed the school, while small laught. Thus source did not have result that is heart the principal, and this things did not easy many things that could down from what their agreement. Made your heart clean, likes at the respomsiblility principal about six mounth have done with health. But if unhealthy could come to emergency unit.while laught. But if this thing happened thus made to destroy, all their creativity undevelop at last come to the leader of institution. All of unhealthy (principal, staff, teacher/tutor). This things would be comfortable and healthy if all of that responsibility have distribution and entrusted with as functional to all system structure organization that at the school. Then the concept have changed, solution, responsible their problem together, and the result have felt as comfortable together for all there are at the environmental. Thi is called with efforted "Benefit" in management operational context, said with decidedness. (F1/A/SMPT/160710/13.00-15.00 wita).

This principal was intelligent and conceptual in an ideas and religious, after this expression be confirmation with others ideas that the vice said that's character as that's true, when principal have met at the others placed. Expression vice as the next;

> Liked that we have seen and felt as a teacher/tutor that have worked with him, the job of principal spread to all function bureaucratic, principal enough given notice and control, however that always given message like things sponsor message. Followed all the point have given and enjoy, as with smile (F1/A/ SMPT/160710/13.00-15.00 wita).

Others ideas from one of the teacher/tutor when still rest, said that; "same idea with this principal have tried with real and all potence power source that involved given believing to the teacher/tutor, however not only to cover its wickness and unable as a leader, could that be done? As look at to rhe research and apologized if wrong, and expressed thi is my idea" (F1/A/ SMPT/160710/13.00-15.00 wita).

This expressed was confirmed with one of the teacher/tutor when still rest as waited the next lesson time. The teacher/tutor said as the next.

> Principal was appreciated others with theirs function and skill, the vice have done all of with responsible and coordination. Principal have given responsibility in their job description, but all of must given back the monitoring and evaluation as its report. Even as internal their school have made teamwork that called "Succeed team" that ech when worked hard foe advancing the school, helped the principal in teamwork, as slmall laugh (F1/A/SMPT/160710/13.00-15.00 wita).

Quality that supported management organization structure at this school have a good and procedural as with model that have given before at the school. For more clear could see at the next table.

Table 3.2. Organization Management Executed Site I at Open Junior
High School (SMP Terbuka) Teratai at Malang Region.

Factor and Dimention	Quality
2. Organization Structure	
a. Efficiency	Principal made job description between vice, teacher/tutor and others teamwork as proportional and professional, divided responsibility, and functional at the school.

b. Model	Always at the vision and mission school done job at the school with full awared, only have not sanction because principal undiscipline, enjoy with any righteous him-self, and given his job to the believer person only.
c. Coordination	Principal have divided the job and responsibility to teachers/tutor, done the job, task and function as the rule have done at the school, created relationship that not "*overlapping*." And made coordination meeting internal and teacher/tutor meeting as priodic or tentative.
d. Benefit power source	Principal made cooperated realatioship that good towards
	and familiar to teacher/tutor, involved teacher/tutor in making process policy school, given free idea, with made activity as familiar, sport together, listen to the preached religion, clean Friday and discussion formal.

The data explained, quality precondition implementation that could support management activity school at the Open Junior High School (SMP Terbuka) Teratai Malang. Have a good enough and this school could develop more, but as substantial still weak especially leadership style the principal that spontaneous adminished the teacher/tutor unconditional. This things made many of ttheirs felt very sad and could seem priority their-self.

If this things unnoticeable would be consequenced of veering of the principal. Impact psicology problem against attitude meekness made to destroy all of the strength that their had. Especially with competence problem that the teacher/tutor have a good quality and quantity, or sustainable at the school needed to repair and more a good planned. That made the main strength and prestation to the school was teacher/tutor that still have "*sense of belonging*" and the high commitment as submission.

c. Development Power Source Management Executed Open Junior High School (SMP Terbuka) Teratai at Malang Region.

See from factor power source, principal, teacher/tutor, staff, instrument physic facility; and finance that school have relative well. As ability managed, principal have skill that managerial and constructive involved from several attitude urgent the leader that have liked intelligent, democration and as soon as taken decision.

Although as quantity that teacher/tutor at thi school still less and not representative if compared with amount of the student, but their efforted and responsible against school sacrifice and submission very high.

Awareness each teacher/tutor at this school enough high, sense of belonging, they proved with performantion and responsible daily against the school. As quality skill teacher/tutor at this school did not same as before, still many teacher/tutor not yet pass certification so that as professi not yet decent to teach, almost all of the teacher/tutor could not do any things at this school "*re-active teaching*" or slow motion, could not use computer and access. As sustainable for short distance still could tolerance but for long distance must "*upgraded*" and "*tune up*" as with requirement and necessary.

Expressed one of the teacher/tutor, when that rest after teaching. The essence of their spoken as the next.

As amount teacher/tutor could say less if compared with amount student that there are, so that still have several honorarium teacher/tutor. With there are honorarium teacher/tutor means school must expensive cost? Thus Government better received the teacher/tutor for this school, so that quality the school could to be well, as their hoped (F1/A/SMPT/150710/13.00-15.00 wita). The others teacher/tutor expressed with enjoy climated, the essence idea as the next.

Teacher/tutor sometimes involved in computer learnt training, internet, english language, and "*e-learning*," but still could not, because busy with a full lesson time and many task that must correction, nevertheless theirs and family have a computer but never wanted to learn, why?...at last back to former, as small laugh and a shame. (F1/B/SMPT/150710/13.00-15.00 wita).

Expressed one of the teacher/tutor, as rest time waited for the next lesson. The essence expressed as the next.

Unique with the teacher/tutor that there are about 10-20% could use computer and able access internet, that others teacher/tutor relative not yet used computer, and access internet. Nevertheless they have learnt at the school or maybe they have not computer at home, and their children also could use the computer. At the school have prepared laptop for teacher/tutor if their needed at the school, learnt computer with free but not always was waited for theirs. Involved facility from school to course english language with enough expensive, but not yet optimal, why? Could you image, how about this school? Now could done, but how about for the future? As small laugh (F1/A/SMPT/150710/13.00-15.00 wita).

Facility that prepared at this school enough good and complete for supporting infrastructure learnt minimal, as laboratorium sciences (physical, chemical and biology), library, instrument learnt class, mosque and facility or canteen/cafetaria school for student buying enough health, a large office-room teacher/tutor about 17 X 9 metres although solid involved principal room about 6 X 7 meters, School Healthy Unit room, Conseling and Guiding room, sports field, Hall used multi-function, or multi-media room only all of not yet efective and efficiency for using or maintenance. Because very weak awared to maintannace. Integrated with finance problem but individual mental that ignore, even without planned the budget and maintenance costat the financial.

As crucial that invented power source at thi school for the teacher/tutor very weak and sad as quantity, quality and the sustainable. Commonly teacher/tutor not professional routinity limit, rituality, formality, that only watching. They did not with a good consentration in learnt process at the school.

facility/infrastructure that prepared not effective even in building process not planned with good, court and open air very narrow, irregular and too many building that have build at the narrow court.

Many finance and cost still less and too many cross finance did not planned but many used others budget for building. Principal only focus for building without quality. Finally as the changed of the principal for the next generation did not as brave as the principal before, how to develop competence teacher/tutor? So could conclusion that power source at this school still not representative. For obviously could see the table as the next.

Table 3.3. Development Power Source Management Executed Site I Open Junior High School (SMP Terbuka) Teratai at Malang Region.

Factor and Dimention	Quality
3. Power Source	
a. Human	As quantity, still diminish lesson teacher/tutor, thus empower honorarium teacher/tutor. As quality, still there are teacher/tutor that not yet pass certification, not yet graduate, many teacher/tutor could not work at the job. So many teacher/tutor that decent to teach.
b. Physic/facility and instrument	As quantity, have complete with any facilty physic and instrument, comfortable class-room for learnt, multimedia room, principal room, have laboratorium sciences, library, learnt media, infrastructure sport. As quality the good condition and ready for use, only from maintannace and useful not yet optimal.
c. Finance/Cost	As quantity enough as with routine budget, contributed from Central Government or region, and from *"generating income."* As quality finance and cost good enough because still less from discipline managed financial so that the condition the *"cash flow"* finance consequences unhealthyful.

d. Management Audit System Executed at Open Junior High School (SMP Terbuka) Teratai at Malang Region.

Research observation result explained about "Management Open Junior High School (SMP Terbuka) in nine years compulsory education," that dimention source information have seen from aspect skill, principal as source audit in saying information management with systematic, intonation that distinct, and follow with body language that convince so that message that said could receive with clear to teacher/tutor. As reference, principal always seek for source information direct from the originil source so that the information could be responsibility. As credibility, principal have had experience that enough a long time as a leader, active in organization formal or nonformal, enjoy with critis ideas, innovative, and wise in managed the school.

From interview result with one of the teacher/tutor in situation relax, enjoy and friendship as the next.

> The beginning that shake hands, laugh and said pleased sitdown, to introduce to the board teachers ….., that our principal "enjoy with this school" means always thought how about with this school? Who's at this school always disccuss, thought and the most advanced the school. Daily that not always seriously, enjoy sport as badminton with their teacher/tutor, like "*refreshing*" togehter, portluck and enjoy also entertainment. As vice or teacher/tutor must fast and advance for school, and sometimes said that "Don't this school have lost from others school, as smile look at the research (F1/A/SMPT/150710/13.00-15.00 wita).

Idea of this teacher/tutor expressed as what there are in situation relax, the essence as the next.

> Principal serious and relax, means sometimes angry, direct called to all of. everywhere did not lost with information about school although as formal at the school, or relax at the school, out of the school, when sport, meeting, activity at the Mosque. He always come at the time and back-home lately almost in the evening, Any time if seen teacher/tutor come late, he given adviced that's bad and seek for the good solution. In contrast if all of lived the school early or have the individual necessary he always given to permit with the true reason and prepared tasks for the student at the class as procedural. Principal always pointed "himself as example before, with serious, and laugh. (F1/A/SMPT/150710/13.00 – 15.00 wita).

> Principal seen from the skill aspect, that in an attitude with confirm comunication; from aspect reference, that information said always from direct source and relevant; and as aspect credibility, principal have believed because have many experience as

a leader of the school. The weakness of the Principal less noticed the style to say the information that hurry and impression arrogant, said information sometimes representative to vice, and still have seen emotional. Solution principal said the information as what there are with not dragged with former given example himself. Conclusion that source comunication have seen from aspect skill have enough clear, aspect reference and aspect credibility enough high, thus quality dimention source comunication enough good and supported management at this school.

Observation result pointed that message that said by principal to the teacher/tutor always noticed several aspect urgent, that's aspect up to date, transformational, clearness, accurate and consistence. Aspct the new one that principal enjoy because have several principle life "more fast more good" and "this day more good than the day before." Like to read, learnt, disccuss with whom. Enjoy watching the news of TV and radio. Asked and seek all of the new information. Aspect transformational, that principal efforted fluently learnt process with requested idea teacher/tutor through meeting to formulate management school. Said the message as soon as and what there are, transparent, and could responsible. Efforted managed information that clear. Aspect clearness, That comunication that have said and given information that objective, distinct, not doubt and representative as with means that have wanted by principal as comunicator. Aspect accurate, that comunication have said to the common with any consideration, accurate, righteous, observer and commitment together, even have ability given information or the fact explanation. Aspect consistence, that comunication principal have said the information as the school vision and mission, constant, and loyal at the rule.

The teacher/tutor expressed that supported, interview when the rainy as the next.

> The good Principal, but if he was angry to all that made fault. He as soon as said the school information everywhere, what there are? And supported this school prestation and inside the teacher/tutor room always said if have advantage followed certification and collected theirs portofolio files even efforted the photocopy cost, as smile and convince. (F1/B/SMPT/150710/ 13.00 – 15.00 wita).

Interview result that principal idea when sat at the his room while drunk coffee, with situation cool of the Air Condition and his vice. The essence spoken as the next.

> I did not doubted more with theirs teacher/tutor, they have known this school principle. The teacher/tutor done satisfy ….all of done with disccuss and speak to others, what else that's for theirs all importance and school …. Let's thought

together, they have motto: worked with full attention, as pointed and watched to motto that hung at the wall. (F1/A/SMPT/150710/13.00-15.00 wita).

If seen from more message, that Principal have said with the new one.
The messaged original and faster, seen from aspect transformational. That message have said fact and transparent. As aspect accurate, message have tested theirs righteous. As aspect consistence, message that have said clear and not change. The weakness, principal otoriter so that message have impressed as instruction, but sometimes the message said by the vice so that made teacher/tutor ignore the message. Principal'solution have said messaged through the letters. Conclusion that commucation source seen from the new aspect enough good, aspect transformational have enough clear, aspect accurate enough clear, and aspect consistence have as that hoped. So that quality dimention message this school comunication enough good and supported school management.

Observatiom result expressed, that advantage media because many media have prepared but did not used and care as optimal even impression. While from interview result with principal when relax at their room and said that "this school have prepared any kind media comunication, only many teacher/tutor that not efforted to use the media because disunderstand and did not learnt." (F1/A/SMPT/150710/13.00-15.00 wita). The teacher/tutor expressed when rest at the teacher/tutor'room, that: "actually we wanted to learn and use media comunication that have prepared at this school but we have not time and tired after teaching." (F1/B/SMPT/150710/13.00-15.00 wita). Media have used the modern technology, the weakness from media comunication that have prepared impression did not useful. The solution of useful the media that have prepared and care at the school as optimal. Conclusion useful and careful the media that prepared at the school not yet optimal.

Observation result expressed, that dimension received message could not know their together. Beside that indication each received the school management process have vision and mission their-self. Interview result with one of the teacher/tutor when at the teacher/tutor room said that: "the teacher/tutor did not known what that principal wanted. Therefore the school have had vision and mission, so that we come to be confusion." (F1/B/SMPT/150710/13.00-15.00 wita). While the others teacher/tutor said the same things that's: "we asked about what that principal have done with vision and mission or not, because that he only build the physic of the school." (F1/A/SMPT/150710/13.00-15.00 wita).

More than all given motivation to teacher/tutor and looking for the right information. The weakness that invented was many different background so that not all could do school management with good. In one means have any perception, solution the received message active in looking for righteous through information that accurately. Seen school management.

Table 3.4. Management Audit System Executed Site I at the Open
Junior High School (SMP Terbuka) Teratai at Malang Region.

Factor and Dimention	Quality
4. Audit	
a. Source	Principal was the expert, used systematic language, intonation distinct, convince language, supported with direct source and orginil, experience, religious, discerment,
b. Message	Message that said with warm and new, from the fact that actually, accurate and careful, as the school vision and mission.
c. Media	supported with many alternative media that prepared and the school had, media easy to find and clean from disturb, with media have reprentative.
d. Received message	a big part could receive message with good.

1.1. Research Invented Executed at Site I at the Open Junior High School (SMP Terbuka) Teratai at Malang Region.

Research invented at Site I at the Open Junior High School (SMP Terbuka) Teratai expressed with research focus, were: Quality condition in school management.

a). School Planned about Management

b). Organization Management.

c). Development Power Source Management.

d). Management Audit System.

Each research focus above, expressed as research invented that detail as the next;

a) School Planned Research Invented about Management Executed Site I at the Open Junior High School (SMP Terbuka) Teratai at Malang Region.

Whole data expressed about school management planned Site I at the Open Junior High School (SMP Terbuka) Teratai at Malang involved; (1) what attitude that must done?; (2) ability to manage; and (3) motivation desired to find the future research invented as the next;

(1) What attitude that must done?

  (a) Principal supported to increase school management.

    (b) Principal build and directed the teacher/tutor.

    (c) Principal seeked for alternative as way out of the problem.

    (d) Principal communication school management.

    (e) Principal changed and asked school management.

(2) Ability Done

    (a) Principal and teacher/tutor done school management.

    (b) Principal efforted convince school management was important and useful for the teacher/tutor.

    (c) Principal believed all of done their job.

    (d) Principal could prove all the job with the fact prestation.

(3) Motivation and Desire

    (a) Principal wanted to sacrifice although moral or material.

    (b) Principal full responsibilty.

    (c) Principal come earlier and back home the last.

    (d) Principal worked with full heart.

    (e) Principal worked with principle and hold his job.

b) Organization Management Research Invented Site I at the Open Junior High School (SMP Terbuka) Teratai at Malang Region.

Whole expressed data about structure organization that supported school management Site I at the Open Junior High School (SMP Terbuka) Teratai at Malang involved; (1) efficiency; (2) model; (3) coordination; and (4) benefit power source could invented research for the future as the next:

(1) Efficiency

    (a) Principal divided the clear job.

    (b) Principal full responsible against school management.

    (c) Principal made a simple oraganization.

    (d) Principal worked with the clear procedure.

(2) Model

    (a) Principal done the task always towards at the school vision and mision.

    (b) Principal always founded at the rule.

    (c) Principal efforted to make a good discipline school.

(3) Coordination

    (a) Principal always done the task with regular and responsibility.

    (b) Principal, vice and teacher/tutor done the task, a good coordinate.

    (c) Principal action with easily, because the clear organization and responsible.

    (d) Principal believed to vice and teacher/tutor with full heart.

(4) Power Source Benefit

    (a) Principal done generation programme to vice and teacher/tutor.

    (b) Principal made functional their with the each responsible.

    (c) Principal involved all of them at the school management.

    (d) Principal given full responsibility to them in action with wise at the school problem.

c) Power Source Development Research Invented Management Executed Site I at the Open Junior High School (SMP Terbuka) Teratai at Malang Region.

Whole data expressed about comunication that supported school management Site I at the Open Junior High School (SMP Terbuka) Teratai at Malang although as quantative or qualitative that involved; (1) human power source that's principal, vice, and teacher/tutor; (2) facility physic and instrument; and (3) source cost could invented research the future as the next.

(1) Human Power Source

    (a) at the basic teacher/tutor at this school still less must seeked for alternative so that find as the needed.

    (b) Principal received honorarium teacher/tutor.

    (c) Principal seeked for teacher/tutor changed that have skill as the needed.

    (d) Principal said the teacher/tutor as academic for increasing knowledge idea.

    (e) Principal facility activity seminar, training and all activity academic.

    (f) Principal made strategy with arranged the teacher/tutor table that same discipline at the teacher/tutor office.

    (g) Principal easily given permit learnt to teacher/tutor.

(2) Facility physic and instrument

  (a) Principal build, repaired, equipment, increased and comfortable all facility instrument that prepared at the school.

  (b) Useful and careful with good all facility instrument that prepared as procedural and discipline.

(3) Cost Source

  (a) Finance source at the routine financial.

  (b) Coorporation official from central Government and region.

  (c) "*Sponsorship*" sometimes.

  (d) Finance added from "*generating income*" school

  (e) Repaired for using school finance priority scale as the budget.

  (f) After using school finance must followed with factur or "invoice".

  (g) Noticed finance out using procedure with agreement from principal, school committee and treasurer.

d). Management Audit System Research Invented Executed Site I at the Open Junior, High School (SMP Terbuka) Teratai at Malang Region.

Entire the expressed data about management audit that supported school management increased competence teacher/tutor site I at the Open Junior High School (SMP Terbuka) Teratai at Malang that involved; (1) source; (2) message; (3) media; (4) received message research invented as the next;

(1) Source

  (a) School management increased competence teacher/tutor have seen from skill aspect communication have supported with material systematic, intonation that distinct and have followed with body language that convince.

  (b) Aspect reference have supported with source a new message that objective, said direct, subject and orginal.

  (c) Aspect credibility have experience and enough long time as the principal, religious, discerment, and decided the school management.

(2) Message

    (a) School management increased competence teacher/tutor have seen from aspect message up to date always said with warm.

    (b) Aspect transformational message that have said from the fact and actually.

    (c) Aspect clearness message that message have said without doubt and really objektive.

    (d) Aspect accurate message that have said with any consideration, accurate, righteous, discuss, observation and commitment that objective.

    (e) Aspect consistence message have said as the school vision and mission.

(3) Media

    (a) School management have seen from aspect prepareness media that supported information and many alternative media that have prepared and school had.

    (b) Aspect have said with easy information that they hoped and free from disturb, likes sound that media result did not disturbed or clean not "*storing*" or "*trouble*," connected with good, to each class all the school with good and easy to access, even used media that have prepared with regular.

    (c) Aspect representative at the all level media what the media have prepared.

(4) Received Message

    (a) School management have seen from believing to a person against the message said different as the heterogen.

    (b) Confident level that did not same interconnect with clearness dimension before.

    (c) Confident level message have said depend at the aspek psicology received, when received the message. What condition of you happy or sad.

    (d) They have abled in receiving message that different or not same one with others, many factor that influence.

    (e) Received message not all could know and receive with good, there are still disccuss with others teacher/tutor as internal when all of them at the office teacher/tutor.

2. Expressed for four focus Data Site II at the Open Junior High School (SMP Terbuka) Tulip at Malang Region.

a. School Planned about Management Executed Site II at the Open Junior High School (SMP Terbuka) Tulip at Malang Region.

Seen from factor attitude school planned that principal the high desired, hoped and responsible against the school, only weakness at the ability to do. The true imaged indirect have seen from several phenomena that appeared and attitude behaviour that daily seem.

As have said one of the teacher/tutor when correction sheet job student as the next.

> Actually principal have efforted with good to do the function, only there are pressed from institution with stick and stiff. So that the action not more optimal but afraid and over careful so impressed doubt and awared in each an action, finally serviced at the school impressed stiff and formal, as laugh (F1/ SMPT/030810/13.00-15.00 wita).

Others thing with idea this teacher/tutor, that; "according principal observation always taken the step safety and managed as the rule and subject not wrong, there are not initiative, as laugh and look at to the research." (F1/SMPT/030810/13.00-15.00 wita).

Attitude planned principal, vice that have done as commonly and teacher/tutor have formed relationship more serviced and formal at the school. For more clear could see the table as the next.

Table 3.5. School Planned about Management Executed Site II at the Open
Junior High School (SMP Terbuka) Tulip at Malang Region.

Factor and Dimension	Quality
1. Attitude Management	
a. What that must done	Principal have attitude managerial, not created relation discriminative, given the fast serviced, suitable, satisfy in serviced, discipline, enjoy substantial than formality, always formal, stiff, beware the style when worked time, made others felt less, instruction principal as the order than the others.
b. Ability	Principal did not worked at the office-room only, enjoy come managed and control the class-room, student and teacher/tutor said greeting, noticed and seen the fact needed, asked direct about complaint their felt at the school, given first example to others, not many speak with pointed example for a good job and proved prestation then given commentary about that job (not in contrast), liked to call and give a good advice direct to the vice, teacher/tutor, or others work-team that about the good or wrong, unhappy drag the job, not easy to give up with the job and worked with entire heart for the school.
c. Motivation and desire	Principal did not must the big dreams, worked what there are and not out of appointed of National Education and institution, worked brave different, not creation and initiative because all of have appointed from institution, start from school vision and mission, and worked with full heart not from ratio.

b. Organization Management Executed Site II at the Open Junior High School (SMP Terbuka) Tulip at Malang Region.

Seen from factor structure organization at this school was bad, principal walked a long, consentration at the institution although vice did not many function at the job only when was needed, have not "*job description*" that clear as worked model. Actually as this school management bureaucratic not over long, relation principal direct to the vice and teacher/tutor. Finally many overlapping job that principal have even teacher/tutor as spontaneous helped the principal'job if seen many and very busy.

Result that spoken with principal when researcher at the office-room, expressed several important information that could be idea reference that: "my job over, advantaged the teacher/tutor always helped me, especially if the school against important activities as school test, national examination, they they helped with freewill, as laugh although seen stress." (F1/SMPT/040810/13.00-15.00 wita).

Idea others teacher/tutor when at the room they said that: principal handle all of without thought to do others job at home or family, different with us, as laugh." (F1/SMPT/040810/13.00-15.00 wita).

Organization structure quality at this school have efficiency, depend at the model as concrete, because amount the teacher/tutor a little thus coordination that done with easy and advantage power source with efficiency. For more clear could see at the table as the next.

Table 3.6. Organization Management Executed Site II at the Open Junior High School (SMP Terbuka) Tulip at Malang Region.

Factor and Dimension	Quality
2. Structure Organization	
a. Efficiency	Principal divided the job to the vice and teacher/tutor as professional and relatives, responsible and coordination, simple organization, done discipline, but constant rational and human-being, as coordinator, done at the school vision and mission, but not cadre teacher/tutor and functional, responsible as the total.
b. Model	Principal always done at the school vision and mission, hold fast the job and awared, there are sanction that clear as the standard, discipline, unhappy with any righteous himself, done the rule, and principal only given the job to the someone that consider able without buildthe others.
c. Coordination	Principal divided the job and responsibility to vice and teacher/tutor, given freely as initiative, autonomy, involved in develop learnt process, done the task and function each as with the rule, done the worked as coordinative between one to the others, so that relationship sustainable and avoid from job overlapping, done coordination meeting internal and teacher/tutor meeting as periodic or tentative.
d. Benefit power source	Principal done relation a good cooperated, towards, realtives, involved all teacher/tutor made process all school activity, given free idea to the teacher/tutor and hurry-up, and school did not made discuss others nonformal.

This invented data if the conclusion that as common quality precondition implementation management that could support managed increasing competence teacher/tutor at the Open Junior High School (SMP Terbuka) Tulip at Malang as whole was bad and unsupported. But if have seen as partial still there are parts that supported managed enhances competence teacher/tutor at the school between others this school still have discipline, responsible, efficiency that have done in behaviour daily as the care of the facility laboratorium computer and sciences (physic, chemical and biology) that have prepared seem still have maintenance with good even they have technician laboratory, not only concept but they also done as consequence. Imperfection of the School could not make to stand for the future. Because all of the planning must changed as total especially "*mind set*" the management institution education. But this prediction ini not for that, certain still there are hoped and opportunity for developing more good though able repaired as management. main key so this school could stand and prestige were teacher/tutor that still have "*sense of belonging*," commitment that high as soul disregard, with supported by confident parent and community.

c. Power Source Develop Management Executed Site II at the Open Junior High School (SMP Terbuka) Tulip at Malang Region.

Seen from factor power source, principal and staff, facility that prepared, and finance/cost that the school have relative not supported, especially if seen from competence teacher/tutor because there are no teacher/tutor that have passed certification, many teacher/tutor that statue have pension but still empower to teach, many teacher/tutor could not use computer, access internet and never read newspaper since many teacher/tutor that leaved information.

Ability teacher/tutor at this school not liked as that imaged before, the fact all the teacher/tutor not yet passed certification, many senior teacher/tutor did not known development and felt "strange" against something; and "*re-active teaching*" or late and like a stupid person. So that if as required professional thus whole the teacher/tutor not yet could teach at the class.

As quantity, amount teacher/tutor still not representative if compared with amount of the student (see document; School Profile Open Junior High School SMP Terbuka Malang year 2010), but efforted and responsible they to the student/school very high, sense of belonging against school not more doubt. As sustainable for short distance optimal but for long distance as soon as must have planned, if not would be dissolved. Institution education of this school have leaved because have lost confident from community.

Expressed one of the tacher/tutor when rest after teaching. Essence spoken that: "as amount teacher/tutor could say less if compared with the student, that's have helped several honorarium teacher/tutor. If thought with there are teacher/tutor honorarium have enough, as smile (F1/SMPT/020811/13.00-15.00 wita).

Expressed others teacher/tutor with climate crowd when rest, idea essence as the next.

Our school have facility laboratorium computer at the room used Air Condition and technician have ready to guide if needed, we free used computer, internet at this school. But we seldom used or advantaged, beside difficult we are very busy with so many worked to correction the task o the student. So felt lazy and veru tired. (F1/SMPT/020810/13.00-15.00 wita).

Facility that have prepared at this school liked laboratorium sciences, computer and multi-media, room/office teacher/tutor enough larger its size about 7 X 8 metres involved principal room with size about 3 X 4 metres, and others room, instrument for learning enough good and equipment for supported infrastructure minimal, involved hall meeting that multi-function (sport), canteen school for student buying seem have enough effective and efficiency in advantage or cleanness, only computer room seldom closed. Infrastructure have enough good, because the school have two person technician/instructor computer that main job as guide to student and teacher/tutor when used involved maintance the computer. They as honorarium that paid from institution.

Financial that prepared from institution only, although how much at the treasure at the school, principal did not known because all of at the institution. This institution very closed and could not mix, school only made process learning. Here financial of the institution made the learnt of this school process sustainable.

Expressed one of the teacher/tutor with situation relax, said many things and essence spoken as the next.

After teaching, with smile and shake hands research,... as the senior teacher/tutor here flurrie, what and wnted where this school the next? Seen fro outside this school enough good but actually ugly,we did not prosperous, small salary, no others earn, but queer this school still continue. This is only awared of the teacher/tutor! High enthusiasm of the teacher/tutor because courage heart (F1/SMPT/020811/13.00-15.00 wita).

As crucial that invented about power source at this school still weak although as quantity, quality and sustainable sad. Commonly they did not professional done process learning only limit routinity, rituality, formality and there are not others alternative. But they actually have the highest enthusiasm and awared as the teacher/tutor. They actually could not consentration with good done the process learnt at the school. As facility/infrastructure that prepared have enough reprentative, arranged and planned with good, even careful. While for finance problem very stick and discipline the benefit, counter institution emphasized at the principle efficiency. For obviously could see at tble as the next.

Table 3.7. Development Power Source Management Executed Site II at the
Open Junior High School (SMP Terbuka) Tulip at Malang Region.

Factor and Dimension	Quality
3. Power Source	
a. Human	As quantity still teacher/tutor, received and empower honorarium teacher/tutor, with amount teacher/tutor at tha begin. As quality still many teacher/tutor that not yet passed certifikation, ungraduate, teacher/tutor could not technology, although teacher/tutor at this school sill have discipline, responsible, consecration, solidarity, sacrifice, awared and commitment that high but still many teacher/tutor that still could not teach.
b. Physic/facility and instrument	As quantity, have completed with any facility physic and instrument the big classroom, clean and comfortable for learnt, multimedia-room, laboratorium sciences, library, learnt media, infrastructure sport. As quality, condition instrument that prepared care with good and ready for using, only from benefit not yet optimal because all care cost guaranteed by institution.
c. Finance/source	As quantitative, have enough that source from "*sponsorship.*" As quality "*cash flow*" finance health because they was discipline, procedural, priority scale, at the needed fact in receiving and expenseas.

d. Management Audit System Executed Site II at the Open Junior High School (SMP Terbuka) Tulip at Malang Region.

See from factor management audit, observation result expressed, that dimension source information have seen from aspect expertness, principal as source comunication that said the information with distinct and convince so the message could receive with clear to the teacher/tutor. Principal not creative about school management since impressed only as ausually. As reference principal only seeked for source information from institution. As credibility, principal have had experience that enough long time as the leader.

Idea from one of the teacher/tutor in situation relax, enjoy and frienship. Essence of the expressed as the next.

> We always met him, shake hand, laugh and said please sit down also introduce to the board teacher/tutor …, that principal done his job and as "right hand" done as target of institution. Institution made decided "almost notihng" strategy that principal could do. Before done at the school, principal have said first to the

institution with several message sponsor. Our school very depend at the strength institution, therefore institution hold a crucial at the ministrative and academic, as with face very sad. (F1/SMPT/020810/13.00-15.00 wita).

Idea others teacher/tutor thi is the right expressed when rest and correction job sheet student. Essence expressed as the next.

> This principal impressed more serious and easy panic if received information anything, if response with fast but sometimes flurrie. Done the job as principal as the usual, beware, impression did not wanted different others school and closed, not fluent at the communication. Communication that have done at the school only limited relation formal each school and not difficult, as looked at to the research with convince (F1/SMPT/020810/13.00-15.00 wita).

Principal idea, when at the office that while drunk fresh water and sign the letter. Essence he said as the next.

> Why the principal always asked something to me about this school management problem, whereas done job as the principal just the same with others principal, there are not different, still many a good school there outside, I did not the queer, but I needed to change, thus when I received letter from Rducation Serviced always I done fully with our teacher/tutor here (F1/SMPT/020810/13.00-15.00 wita).

Excess principal have seen from aspect expertness, that comunication always response with fast each policy that decided by institution. Aspect reference, the information that have said always from institution direct. As aspect credibility, principal have believed because the experience and as confident fully from institution. The weakness of the principal inclined stiff and not creative at the leader. Solution principal must be cared discipline and did not chosen love, have done teacher/tutor. Conclusion that source comunication have seen from aspect expertness enouh clear, aspect reference right and aspect credibility enough high, thus quality dimension source comunication at this school enough good and supported managed enhanced competence teacher/tutor.

Observation result pointed the message that have said from principal to the teacher/tutor always noticed several aspect crucial, that's aspect up to date, transformational, clarity, accurate and consistence.

Aspect up to date, that actually principal have had initiative but said information to the teacher/tutor must be discussed and requested agreement institution. Aspect transformational, that school decided policy at the needed fact, have said message as soon as and what there are, transparent and could be responsibility. Aspect clarity, that message have had said as objective, stiff, not doubt and representative as the message that desired. Aspect accurate, the comunication that have said from principal with full consider, accurate and true. Aspect consistence, the message that have said from principal information done at the school vision and mission.

Interview result with the teacher/tutor when rainy and after the others teacher/tutor teaching, said that: "principal always communication all information same suitable with what that have said from institution. He honest but stiff, did not done something." (F1/SMPT/020810/13.00-15.00 wita).

Interview result more expressed, that teacher/tutor idea when sat at the teacher/tutor office, as idea with others teacher/tutor expressed: "principal difficut for have given input about information that have said from institution." (F1/SMPT/020810/13.00-15.00 wita).

If seen from over message that have said principal as the up to date, that message was that true. Seen from aspect transformational, the message that have said as the fact at the school. As aspect accurate, message have tested the correctness. As aspect consistence, message that have said with clear and without changed. The weakness, principal inclining authoritative so the message that have said inpressed as the order that must be done but seldom message that have said always late because waited the agreement from institution. Solution principal must seldom comunication and made a good relationship with institution and education serviced that with the teacher/tutor or with others principal. Conclusion that source communication have seen from aspect up to date enough good, aspect transformational enouh clear, aspect accurate enough clear and aspect consistence have the hoped. So the quality dimension message communication at this school enough good and supported managed increased competence teacher.

Observation result expressed, that this school have had media communication that's good but th benefit less optimal because feared wrong. According interview result with teacher/tutor when relax at the office said that: "actually with media that have prepared at this school free for using but because there are procedure that clear that if media used with the wrong way, we must changed ourself. So that we afraided to use the media." (F1/SMPT/020810/13.00-15.00 wita). Parallel with that, others teacher/tutor expressed at the same room that: "this school have not financial maintenance for it instrument even financial have not budgeted for buying a new instrument, so that we very cared of there are." (F1/SMPT/020811/13.00-15.00 wita). Excess the media that have prepared to use the modern technology. The weakness from media communication have prepared at this school since impressed unseful. Solution maximal used media that there are and cared as professional. Conclusion that media that have used at the school still not yet optimal.

Observation result expressed, that dimension received message, as average received the message with good by bthe teacher/tutor. One of the teacher/tutor when at the teacher/tutor room said that: "all of the information we have received from principal and have known and what that principal said must be done, although we did not agreed with that decision." (F1/SMPT/020810/13.00-15.00 wita). Parallel with idea others teacher/tutor, expressed that: "we as the teacher/tutor awared our tasked and compulsory at this school, thus all we done as with principal hoped." (F1/SMPT/020810/13.00-15.00 wita). Excess the teacher/tutor more discipline and always done the policy. The weakness that have met each policy school ultimate done by each teacher/tutor. The Solution apply and continuously discipline each time to whom without chosen love. Seen from dimension teacher/tutor as received message that communication still less supported policy at this school.

Table 3.8. Management Audit System Executed Site II at the Open Junior High School (SMP Terbuka) Tulip at Malang Region.

Factor and Dimention	Quality
4. Audit	
a. Source	Not yet supported by the expert principal in comunication, although have supported by language that systematic, inovation that distinct, stiff, have not followed with language body that convince, source message direct, not yet experience whereas have a long time as the principal, religious, energetic, fast, suitable and ripe in communication.
b. Message	Message not always said with "*up to date*," the message was said with warm, fact, accurately and righteous with the school vision and mission.
c. Media	Supported with many alternative media, media that free from disturb and easy to find, and the media have representative.
d. Receive message	Message could know and receive with good to all of the teacher/tutor.

2.1. Research Invented Executed Site II at the Open Junior High School (SMP Terbuka) Tulip at Malang Region.

Research invented at site II at the Open Junior High School (SMP Terbuka) Tulip at Malang expressed as the sequence research focus, were; condition quality in done management school.

a). School Plannned about Executor

b). Organization Executor.

c). Development Power Source Management Executor.

d). Manajemen Audit System.

Each research focus above, describe as research invented that detail as the next;

a) **Research Invented Planned School about Executed Site II at the Open Junior High School (SMP Terbuka) Tulip at Malang Region.**

As the whole expressed data about planned school Site II at the Open Junior High School (SMP Terbuka) Tulip at Malang involved; (1) What attitude that must done; (2) Ability to do; and (3) Desire Motivation could in the front of the research invented as the next:

(1) What attitude that must done
   (a) Principal supported to help school management.
   (b) Principal build and strive for teacher/tutor.
   (c) Principal seeked for alternative as way out the problem.
   (d) Principal changed and asked about management school.
   (e) Principal made society management school.

(2) Ability to do
   (a) Principal and teacher/tutor managed management school.
   (b) Principal efforted convince management school was crucial and benefit for teacher/tutor.
   (c) Principal confidented by all person to do.
   (d) Principal could prove all work result with prestation that fact.
   (e) Apply distinctness with sanction that clear.

(3) Desire and Motivation
   (a) Principal wanted sacrifice although moral or material.
   (b) Principal full responsibility.
   (c) Principal come earlier and back home the last.
   (d) Principal worked with full heart and soul.
   (e) Principal worked with principle as the confided.

b) **Research Invented Organization Executed Site II at the Open Junior High School (SMP Terbuka) Tulip at Malang Region.**

As the whole expressed data about structure organization that supported management school Site II at the Open Junior High School (SMP Terbuka) Tulip at Malang involved: (1) efficiency; (2) model; (3) coordination; and (4) benefit power source could in front research invented as the next:

(1) Efficiency

    (a) Principal divided the job with clear.

    (b) Principal full responsibility against management school.

    (c) Principal made the simple organization .

    (d) Principal worked with procedure with clear.

(2) Model

    (a) Principal made all the task always done at the clear school vision and mission.

    (b) Principal always pledged at the rule.

    (c) Principal efforted to make a good shool discipline.

    (d) Principal bewared with heavy sanction from institution if happened the wrong way in doing the task.

(3) Coordination

    (a) Principal done the task always regular action and responsibility.

    (b) Principal, vice and teacher/tutor done the task, with good coordination.

    (c) Organization and responsible that clear made easy principal in action.

    (d) Principal made full confidence to vice and teacher/tutor with intentions.

(4) Benefit Power Source

    (a) Principal made their functional with each responsible.

    (b) Principal made all their integrated decided the management school.

    (c) Principal given their full responsible in action the school problem statesmanship.

    (d) Principal applied discipline that same against all the teacher/tutor without made different one to each others.

c) Research Invented Development Power Source Management Executed Site II at the Open Junior High School (SMP Terbuka) Tulip at Malang Region.

As the whole expressed data about communication that supported managed management school site II at the Open Junior High School (SMP Terbuka) Tulip at Malang although as quantative or qualitative that involved: (1) power source humankind as the principal and teacher/tutor; (2) physic facility and instrument; and (3) finance source could in the front of the research invented as the next.

(1) Humankind Power Source
   (a) as the basic teacher/tutor at this school still less must be seeked for alternative so could as the needed.
   (b) Principal received teacher/tutor than used teacher/tutor pension from institution.
   (c) Principal seeked for teacher/tutor changed that have skill as their needed.
   (d) Principal called all the teacher/tutor as academic to increase their scientific.
   (e) Principal made facilitation activity seminar, training and all academic activity.
   (f) Principal made strategy with arranged the teacher/tutor table and same knowledge at the office.
   (g) Principal made easy to give permit learnt to the teacher/tutor.
   (h) Changed bought a package book as the invoiced.

(2) Physic Facility and Instrument
   (a) Principal build, repaired, equipped, added and comfortable all facility instrument that prepared at the school.
   (b) Benefit and care with good all facility instrument that prepared as procedural and discipline.
   (c) empower procedure that stick and emphasized at responsible the user facility instrument.

(3) Finance Source
   (a) Fund source at the financial rountine budget.
   (b) Fund from central government and region.
   (c) Seeked for "Sponsorship" seldom and closed theirself.
   (d) Fund added from "generating income" school
   (e) Repaired to use school treasure especially scale priority as the budget that have decided.
   (f) Each user treasure have proved with invoiced and factur that bought.
   (g) Made noticed procedure user treasure that paid as the agreement from institution.

d). Research Invented Management Audit System Site II at the Open Junior High School (SMP Terbuka) Tulip at Malang Region .

As the whole expressed data about audit that supported managed management school increased competence teacher/tutor site II at the Open Junior High School (SMP Terbuka) Tulip at Malang that involved; (1) source; (2) message; (3) media; (4) receive message could in the front research invented as the next;

(1) Source

    (a) Principal direct said message to the teacher/tutor.

    (b) Principal said announcement with any way: pronounciation at the teacher/tutor room, when homage, letter at the meeting.

    (c) Have said the principle message what there are as the letter.

(2) Message

    (a) Message have said as soon as and not dragged.

    (b) Message source at the clear fact.

    (c) Message have accurate before and riped.

    (d) Message not out off from vision and mission.

(3) Media

    (a) Media have done through loudspeaker, blackboard, discuss, SMS although not all of, and e-mail not yet used.

    (b) Efforted media that ready for use.

(4) Received Message

    (a) Teacher/tutor responded with good.

    (b) Teacher/tutor could could do with good..

    (c) Teacher/tutor seeked for others information.

    (d) Teacher/tutor called discuss with others teacher/tutor at the office.

3. Expressed Four Focus Data Site III at the Open Junior High School (SMP Terbuka) Mawar at Malang Region.

a. School Planned about Executed Open Junior High School (SMP Terbuka) Mawar at Malang Region.

Seen from factor attitude planned menagement have happened not efficiency because all system have not efficiency and representative even inclining not done more. Management that done as routine that task daily as teacher/tutor and reponsible profession, yet as ministrative have not done or function more. This school done without the clear menagement, relation structure organization confused, happened groups between that pro and contrast with principal, happened like and dislike, teacher/tutor have not cared what the principal said because they have not believed to the principal of that school, since principal could not do anything against that daily theirs.

Proved when principal and research was spoken at the principal'room when the rest time about 12.00 – 13.00 wita there are one senior sport teacher/tutor that said with loud voice and emotional to move the car in the front of the principal without said sorry. Since principal was angry and said sorry to the research. The research could not think how bad attitude the teacher/tutor to their principal.

Principal have not known more what that must done especially with the teacher/tutor problem, impressed principal flurrie against all the teacher/tutor. Because between they have not emphatic how much harmonize, they made each others not to honour. Relationship between their have not clear, not formal more, not honour to each others, and impressed all of without rule.

This phenomenon have read in expression of the principal when at the work room expressed as the next.

> Actually principal all of wrong against the teacher/tutor here 'what must be done?' whereas if principal wanted to move their he could do, but principal 'still thinking and not with his heart' maybe principal youngest than their, and principal awared that I was not from this city, then how about for it solution? Principal back request for the idea, as smile and bow down his head (F1/SMPT/090810/13.00-15.00 wita).

This things be strong by one of the teacher/tutor with made their excused because when the event they are overthere and said as the next.

> Nah that's attitude teacher/tutor against their principal without honour and polite, against the teacher/tutor just the same, could you image if there are guest

as the research, once more we are said to apology. But the fact that there are at the our school, principal was smile as bowdown his head. (F1/SMPT/090810/13.00-15.00 wita).

This expression made distinct again bu one of the teacher/tutor when they are relax while was waited the next lesson time and said as this next.

As the parent that's the actually attitude teacher/tutor here especially again as the senior teacher/tutor. Whereas must be not liked that, did their? He asked to the research. But that's not wrong at all to the teacher/tutor here because principal did not closed their with full at the several activity and not distinct in action, as laugh convince. (F1/SMPT/090810/13.00-15.00 wita).

Ironic again when research at the teacher/tutor room and spoken with the teacher/tutor, then the principal come and said with one of the teacher/tutor where overthere, infact many others teacher/tutor that said; "what did he wanted to enter at this room, as looked at to each other and impressed why must he come here?." Even there are between teacher/tutor that said "approach maybe?" or "because wanted to apology as the principal," not appreciated and come, did not have climated friendship.

Ability principal done each management school very weak. One of the teacher/tutor when after teaching and said as the next.

Virtually this Principal have known about management and ever studied management education graduated programme, only when the practical could not implication. Principal over felt and not clear, however the leader must have art, as looked at convince to research. (F1/SMPT/100810/13.00-15.00 wita).

Others teacher/tutor when rechecked result job sheet student at the teacher room said that: "that principal have not established and distinctness as the leader, he was leaded more many with conscience not with rasio so over flow from the leader, as small laugh as the leader have fault." (F1/SMPT/100810/13.00-15.00 wita).

Expressed others teacher/tutor at the same time said as the next.
Principal must be leaded this school out of that system not at the desire of the teacher/tutor so finally brought with his system, so difficult could requirement all desire the teacher/tutor, however the action rational thus happened "yes or no" in action of the leader, said as laugh as principal have fault. (F1/SMPT/100810/13.00-15.00 wita).

Consequence from leader attitude that have had the principal seem very difficult to do the motivation and desired to advance this school. Others teacher/tutor expressed as the next.

> Relation organization between principal with teacher/tutor at this school have not harmony and not health again, however principal have desired and the high motivation to advance this school, as teacher/tutor have not supported more each programme that principal have given, as small laugh. (F1/SMPT/100810/13.00-15.00 wita).

Interconnecting with that idea, others teacher/tutor said that: "leadership principal our school really have no more again, even did not hoped many about advancing this school as long as principal still at this school, as laugh convince and impressed annoying." (F1/SMPT/100810/13.00-15.00 wita).

Accoding others teacher/tutor have said that: "relationship between principal with teacher/tutor here have 'not connected again' means have happened the groups, brought each desire, and principle their that important not happened each loss even call to seek for each weak, they said with loud laugh." (F1/SMPT/100810/13.00-15.00 wita).

Attitude managed bureaucratic between principal and teacher/tutor at this school have not real again and happened relation distrust to each others even have walked each others. Did not found serviced that as the usuallu formal as the institution the commonly school all of awlked with their awareness and their important rule and discipline school inclining ignored. For more clear could see at the table as the next.

Table 3.9. School Planned about Executed Open Junior High School (SMP Terbuka) Mawar at Malang Region.

Factor and Dimension	Quality
1. Attitude Managed	
a. What that must do	Principal did not efforted to apply attitude managerial with good even felt fllurrie to handle the problem at this school, still believed history from forefather (mitos) and managed the management instrumentsnational test for the student, likes; pencil, eraser, ruller that convince could make fluently at the test their impact against the passed of the student test, recreated relation discriminative that very hard at the teacher/tutor group or principal. Efforted to give a good service but in practical not satisfied and not yet abled to change relationship formal to be nonformal.
b. Ability managed	Principal managed management school did not supported at the attitude the good managerial, many that have worked at the table and with Air Condition room, not abled to give easiness and way out as alternative espeacilly problem to senior teacher/tutor, did not called and given, direct towards teacher/tutor but vice always done the right or the wrong of the teacher/tutor, not yet done any kinds *manuver* that able made fast the school changed, worked with half heart and soul so that impressed still seked for confident as the leader.
c. Motivation and desire	Principal did not made the motivation with clear because still flurrieness brought vision and mission school, did not different at the creation or initiative as health not yet as coordinator managed that able given towards, controller and assessment to teacher/tutor, did not done at the vision and mission school with good, and did not applied principle work with heart.

b. Organization Executed Open Junior High School (SMP Terbuka) Mawar at Malang Region.

Seen from factor structure organization at this school defficiency, involved from coordination and responsible of the principal to vice and all of the teacher/tutor "*job description*" was not coordination and done, so that relationship one to each other not at the function again, between principal with vice or staff did not harmony, they worked each own without model that have done so difficult to responsibility.

Result spoken with principal when at the office, how important several information that could do reference as the next.

I could work only with young and want to work person example there are several teacher/tutor that still young, more fast, more fresh in thinking, even for advancing this school they very consent spent their time for the school with comitment they 'very high,' with their smile. (F1/SMPT/100810/13.00-15.00 wita).

Expressed that made strong this idea the other teacher/tutor said as the next.

> Many policy that they unknown 'when thatb things have spoken' in the board teacher/tutor? Seem that thins only as the decision only from principal. Queer again when that must be done as principal wanted so tha's no more coordination or organization and that there are only 'each indeed' that far from creativity leader or group, that he only laugh, sad and a little emotional. (F1/SMPT/100810/13.00-15.00 wita).

Expressed that almost same and at once distincted before said as the next.

> Did not mistaken this school the real many teacher/tutor that frustration because never felt the comfortable climate and safe, did not had the warm climate learn. Teacher/tutor never be used and benefit as optimal at the police principal, as laugh and seem sad (F1/SMPT/100810/13.00-15.00 wita).

If have seen from aspect structure organization that have done at this school not efficient more, seen from from all relation or organization function unhealthy, all impression natural and the rule or discipline almost have not done more. For more clearly could see at the table as the next.

Table 3.10. Management Organization at Open Junior High
School (SMP Terbuka) Mawar at Malang Region.

Factor and Dimention	Quality
2. Structure Organization	
a. Efficiency	Principal have given the job to vice and teacher/tutor with clear although not yet professional and not responsibity proved in practical still worked himself, have not ability made simple bureaucracy as professional, could not apply discipline as fast but more emotional, could not do as coordinator that responsibility against mechanism school management that professional and proportional, not done at the vision and mission school with good and not yet made functional all staff of the school.

b. Model	Principal done management school not full at the vision and mission school, unawared, unclear the standard sanction, undiscipline, enjoy with true himself, used the rule, only given the task to someone that consider able without building the others.
c. Coordination	Principal given the job and responsibility to vice and teacher/tutor, given free as initiative, autonomy, but in practical not done because have not supported, not yet done the task and each function as the rule, not able done the job as coordinative between a field with others, so still many job overlapping, sometimes made internal coordination meeting and teacher/tutor meeting.
d. Benefit power source	Principal not able made relationship corperation with good, towards, relationship to the teacher/tutor made processing all the school activity, given free to the teacher/tutor ideas, and school have not made activity that relationship as saving relationship, sport together, discuss nonformal et cetera.

Conclusion of the describes that as commonly quality management could support each increased competency teacher/tutor at the school, if have not supported the school would be broken. Because community was leaved consequence loss their believer even would more very terrible if teacher/tutor that "leaved" the school. As psychology maybe it could happen because any pressure or school environmental created that have not conducive again (destructive).

c. Development Power Source Management Executed Open Junior High School (SMP Terbuka) Mawar Kota Malang Region.

Seen from factor power source, although humankind or the teacher/tutor, facility that prepared; and budget that school'had enough relative. If as quantity that teacher/tutor here still less and not yet representative if compared with total student, but effort and responsibility with their awared to student very high their sacrifice or subordination.

Awared each teacher/tutor at this school was low, their sense of belonging against school'advanced was low could prove with their daily performance and resposiblity. Only a certain teacher/tutor that have enthusiasm, wanted and that high commitment. As quality teacher/tutor'ability at this school that have imaged before, still many teacher/tutor that not yet passed certification so as profession have not taught, could not use computer and access internet (informatica technology) et cetera. As sustainable for a short distance still could tolerance but for a long distance must "*upgraded*" and "*tune up*" as with demand and requisites levels.

Expression one of the teacher/tutor, when that was rested after teaching, essence of their spoken as the next.

Actually we still less of the teacher/tutor because between total student and teacher/tutor not balance more its rasio so we have many teacher/tutor honorary and consequence we must seeked for its honorarium, and than process learning could do with good. That's still many teacher/tutor that have two or three lessons each teacher/tutor, actually heavy for me as we hoped have an ideal from goverment." (F1/SMPT/090810/13.00-15.00 wita + document).

Expression others teacher/tutor with crowd climate and unhappy, essence that's: "I have taught for a long time double lessons as History (PKn) and relighion (Agama), actually heavy for me but never mind because have not teacher/tutor could change, as smile and shame." (F1/SMPT/090810/13.00-15.00 wita).

Expression one of the teacher/tutor, when rested after teaching said the next.

At this school sometimes made training computer as internal for teacher/tutor, we have permitted, but only a little wanted to learn. Even I am as teacher/tutor TIK (Informatica Technology and Computer) as himself called theirs but did not, principle of they did not "beneficial" for theirself thus did not followed at the infrastructure their have. Only 4 – 5 persons only have done the IT (Informatica Technology), said with laugh and felt queer (F1/SMPT/090811/13.00-15.00 wita).

Opportunity that same others teacher/tutor supported expression above, this the next.

Teacher/tutor here could want to learn that a new like computer and internet very difficult, only certainly teacher/tutor that wanted to learn especially for young teacher/tutor still have commitment. But if called for eating together at this school all of with faster, as laugh and seen to others (F1/SMPT/090810/13.00-15.00 wita).

Facility that have prepared at this school enough good and complete for supporting infrastructure learnt minimal, like science laboratory (physical, chemical and biology), library, instruments for learning at the class, mosque and facility, canteen/cafetaria school for student enough health, office teacher/tutor big size 8 X 9 meters although namun full included Principal'office its size 4 X 7 meters, health office, Guiding and Counseling office, sport hall, aula meeting and multi-media office all of not yet effective and efficiency its maintance and useful. Since all of the instruments damaged, because have not used. Without planning about its maintance budget, individual disregard and neglect.

The finance from committee school government. Power source that very weak as quantity, quality and sad its sustainanble. At the commonly they not professional made process learning only routine, rituality, formality and have not others alternative. This school done only from apart of the teacher/tutor. They done the process learning with forced and could not with a good concentration. As infrastructure facility that prepared as physic, not arrange with good, not useful /operational as optimal and not cared with good. About budget or finance very limited and its useful not efficiency even not clear. Seen the table as the next.

Table 3.11. Development Power Source Management Executed Open
Junior High School (SMP Terbuka) Mawar at Malang Region.

Factor and Dimension	Quality
3. Power Source	
a. Human	As quantity, this school still less the teacher/tutor at the certain lesson like religion thus principal have received and empower teacher/tutor history lesson with cover three lessons, beside that received teacher/tutor honorarium. As quality still many teacher/tutor not yet past certification, not yet graduate, teacher/tutor without anything although still have discipline, responsibility, dedication, solidarity, sacrifice, awared and commitment that high but still many teacher/tutor impress confused against our duty and task because principal could not effort and have not attitude managerial.
b. Physic/facility and instrument	As quantity, have enough and complete with any instrument and facility physic a big classroom, clean and comfort for learning, multimedia room, science laboratory, library, media learning, sport infrastructure. As quality, condition a good instrument that have prepared and ready for used, only from useful not yet optimal and impress nothing at all because have not a special power like technisi and labourer. Although there are teacher/tutor that have pointed to handle and responsible, about the facility but have not done effective, this things because have not budget for maintenance.
c. Finance/source	as quantitative, have done enough that source from routine finance and central government finance or region. As quality finance and budget this school not discipline at the executor so "*cash flow*" condition unheatlh, because have not discipline thus creditor for not its budgeting.

d. Manajemen Audit System Open Junior High School (SMP Terbuka) Mawar at Malang Region.

Seen from management audit factor, the invented from observation result that dimension source information have seen from expert aspect, principal as source communication said policy information have efforted with sistimatic although not clear and with able to convince, so teacher/turor received the message with enjoy. As reference, principal have efforted to look for source information that could responsibilty. As credibility, principal have not experience that long time enough and there are teachers/tutors at this school have wanted for doing management school. According observation result with ourself felt could not do this things when we said the office, the essence as the next.

> Very complex the problem at this school, however have efforted for along time to seek for the solution so this teacher/tutor must together, unity but in fact more difficulty. As a principal unhappy with attitude group, however they have senior, experience and fath but like not understood person. If wanted with honesty to bring very difficult actually school mision, have our burden that different with the others school. How about you? School request respon as with a little laugh (F1/SMPT/090810/13.00-15.00 wita).

One of the teacher/tutor said dan expressed the essence, that: "school concept must different with there are concepts, included principal, teacher/tutor, student and all stakeholder, but in fact at this school have not reflected the faith as religious, I felt queer and have met here a broken comunication." (F1/SMPT/090810/13.00-15.00 wita).
Other idea said by one of the teacher, essence expressed as the next below.

> No others that could make back unity the teacher at this school, if principal with his responsibility, ability as stead fast and immovable leader, this is that we sad as the teacher/tutor with smile, this school going on with our owner (F1/SMPT/040810/13.00-15.00 wita).

Principal have at aspect expert, that in comunication and relation that enough good and as emotional have touched. Aspect reference, the information have said that relevant with it source. As aspect credibility, emotional toched of principal in comunication have good. Principal weakness not distinct and communicative in communication. Solution from principal have said the information as with good approached, although needed a long time. Conclusion that source communication have seen from aspect expert not clear, aspect reference not right and aspect credibility was low, thus quality dimension source communication at this school not supported and good managed the teacher/tutor increased competence management.

Observation result pointed the message that have said from principal to the teacher/tutor always noticed several crucial aspect, that aspect up to date, transformational, clarity, accurate and consistence. Aspect up to date, distinctive that principal have not ability because not teacher/tutor that supported and not active asked and seek for a new information. Aspect transformational, distinctive that principal not factual in formula management school, not transparant and could not responsibility. Aspect clarity, distinctive the comunication that have said not objective, not distinct and not representative. Aspect accurate, the comunication that have said not consider as accurate, careful and commitment that clear. Aspect consistency, distinctive the comunication that have said by principal its information not harmonious with school vision and mission and unconsistence.

From observation have ordered that principal, when others teacher/tutor after teaching said that: "what information that have said by principal we have not believed, even asked the righteousness." (F1/SMPT/090810/13.00-15.00 wita). This expression acquitted with the others teacher/tutor at the teacher/tutor' room said that: "as much information that principal have said, as much that much that must we asked about the rightousness of the information." (F1/SMPT/090810/13.00-15.00 wita). Others side this expression all of have unbieleved to the principal more, better be changed with that efforted to get back the school condition to be normal." (F1/SMPT/090810/13.00-15.00 wita).

If we seen from the weakness ordered that principal have said as the new one, that always efforted to do the original. Seen from aspect transformational, that principal always efforted to look for order at the base at the fact condition and transparent. As aspect accurate, at the bsed message that have said its right. As aspect consistence, message that have said sometimes changed. As principal weakness, have not made the clear sanction and not as optimal wanted to repair and self-evaluation, even impression more appreciated attitude. Principal'solution have said the message through the letters, vice announcement for saying the message to the teacher/tutor. Conclusion that source communication have seen from aspect the new that message unresponsibility and bad. As aspect transformational that the message enough clear. For aspect clarity that the uncertain message, as from aspect consistence that the message not as school vision and mission that be hoped. So quality dimension message communication at this school not good and not supported school management.

Expression basic observation result, that benefit media communication at this school based have prepared but not used as optimal that impression not cared. As from observation result with principal when relax at the room that have said: "our school have prepared anykind media communication, only many teacher/tutor that not efforted to use the media because not understood, not wanted to learn and appreciate against the school." (F1/SMPT/090810/13.00-15.00 wita). That others teacher/tutor expression when that relax at the teacher/tutor'room, that: "we did not want to benefit media at this school, because beside the media many that broken, principal felt decent and each competitor." (F1/SMPT/090810/13.00-15.00 wita).

Most media there are used modern technology. As weakness from media communication that have prepared at the school not representative, impression not cared. Conclusion media that used at the school not optimal.

Expression based observation result, that reciver dimension message have not received and each others receiver message that policy have vision and mission theirself. One of teacher/tutor based observation result when at the room'teacher/tutor said that: "we as the teacher/tutor did not know about what principal wanted, although we known this school vision and mission, and we did not understand with principal-self wanted." (F1/SMPT/090810/13.00-15.00 wita). As others teacher/tutor said with the same things that: "we did not want to ask about what principal have not done as the school vision and mission sekolah, at the based we did not care more, up to him." (F1/SMPT/090810/13.00-15.00 wita).

Most without communication between principal with teacher/tutor, but with high awareness of the teacher/tutor done our tasks and duty as with good each responsibility. Teacher/tutor awareness based with our religious and faith, as human being theirs still have conscious and responsibility professional. Weakness where invented of teacher/tutor since refuse with distinct all the message policy that principal have said, so principal have lost his as a leader at this school. Solution must have the third human that efforted to handel as formal or education service for making this school with professional manner. Conclusion did not have message that could receive and do by teacher/tutor at this school.

Table 3.12. Management Audit System Open Junior High
School (SMP Terbuka) Mawar Malang Region.

Factor and Dimension	Quality
4. Audit	
a. Source	Principal enough expert in communication but did not support with dictinct and clear language body convince, support with source message that direct objective and original, not experience but regilious, energetic but not yet done to make policy.

b. Message	Principal have said the message with good but did not up to date, message sometimes have said different fron the actual fact, clarity message still not clear and not objectify, message that have said not yet consider with clear, and the message did not as the school vision and mission.
c. Media	Media that have belonged, have supported many alternative school communication media, media have said with easy information that have hoped and free from disturb voice, and media have representative.
d. Receiver message	Message have received with good to the teacher/tutor, although still several teacher/tutor not yet so that many question about the message.

3.1. Research Invented at the Open Juniour High School (SMP Terbuka) Mawar Malang Region.

Research invented at the Open Junior High School (SMP Terbuka) Mawar Malang region as the research focus, were: Quality condition at the management school.

- a). School'planned about management.
- b). Management organization.
- c). Development source power management.
- d). Management audit system.

Each research focus, described at the research invented that detail as the next;

a). Planned Research Invented School about Management Open Junior High School (SMP Terbuka) Mawar Malang Region.

From the all described data about planned school Open Junior High School (SMP Terbuka) Mawar Malang region included: (1) what attitude must be done?; (2) ability for doing; and (3) desire motivation as the front of research invented as the next:

(1) What attitude must be done?
  - (a) Principal have not supported at the school management.
  - (b) Principal have not guided and helprd the teacher/tutor.
  - (c) Principal have not looked for alternative as way out from the problem.
  - (d) Principal have not changed and asked about school executed management.
  - (e) Principal always used vice as the relationship to the teacher/tutor.

(2) Ability for doing

    (a) Principal have not supported by the all teacher/tutor done the school management.

    (b) Principal efforted to convince the school executed management was urgent and benefit for the teacher/tutor.

    (c) Principal have not believed by the all teacher/tutor for doing school management.

    (d) Principal have not proved all work result with fact prestation.

    (e) Weak in desire, ability, and comitment principal in leader the school.

(3) Motivation and desire

    (a) Principal have not sacrificed although moral or material to advance the school.

    (b) Principal have not responsibility fulfill against the school.

    (c) Principal sometimes come ealier and back sometimes more fast without news.

    (d) Principal have not done with fully prepared.

    (e) Principal have done with prinsiple as responsibility have received the jobs.

b). Research Invented Organization Management Open Juniour High School (SMP Terbuka) Mawar Malang Region.

Principle all the described data about structure organization that supported school management Open Juniuor High School (SMP Terbuka) Mawar Malang region, included: (1) efficiency; (2) model; (3) coordination; and (4) benefit source power could make the front of research invented as the next:

(1) Efficiency

    (a) Principal have divided job-describe with clear.

    (b) Principal have given fulfill responsibility to the teacher/tutor.

    (c) Principal made organization simple.

    (d) Principal have not worked with clear procedure.

(2) Model

    (a) Principal have done all the job as the clear school vision and mission.

    (b) Principal have not founded on at the rule.

    (c) Principal have not made discipline at the good school vision and mission.

(3) Coordination

    (a) Principal have done the job but irregular and unresponsibility.

    (b) Principal, vice, and teacher/tutor have done their jobs, but without coordinate even as organization not at their function.

    (c) Organization and responsibility not clear so made difficult principal done.

    (d) Principal have not made full believeness to vice and teacher/tutor.

(4) Benefit source power

    (a) Principal have not made their functional as each responsibility.

    (b) Principal have not integrated their staff to make their school management.

    (c) Principal have not given full responsibility to their staff in action at the school problem.

    (d) Principal have not done the same discipline against all teacher/tutor.

    (e) Principal have not done programme generation to their teacher/tutor.

c). Research Invented Development Source Power Executed Management Open Junior High School (SMP Terbuka) Mawar Malang Region.

Principle all described data about communication that have supported executed management school site III at Open Junior High School (SMP Terbuka) Mawar Malang region although as quantative or qualitative that included: (1) source power human although principal and teacher/tutor; (2) facility physic and instruments; and (3) source finance could be front in research invent as the next.

(1) Human power source

    (a) The based teacher/tutor at this school still less must be looked for alternative so that as with their needed.

    (b) Principal made to be the definite teacher/tutor.

    (c) Principal looked for the changer teacher/tutor that have a skill that same as their needed.

    (d) Principal said to their teacher/tutor as academic to increase about their skill.

    (e) Still have teacher/tutor taught for three different lessons.

    (f) Principal done seminar activity, training and all academic activity.

    (g) Principal made strategy with the seat of the same skill teacher/tutor at the teacher/tutor'room.

    (h) Principal made to give permit to learn to their teacher/tutor.

(2) Facility physic and instrument

    (a) Principal have not build, repaired, added and comfortable all facility instrument at the school.

    (b) Principal said to the teacher/tutor to use and care with good all facility instrument at the school.

(3) Source financial

    (a) Fund source at routine finance.

    (b) Fund from government centre and region.

    (c) Look for "Sponsorship".

    (d) Added fund from "generating income" school

    (e) Repaired to use financial school have not used as scala priority as the budget.

    (f) Each used finance have not proved with "invoice" bought.

    (g) Noticed prosedure finance used have not with who have agreed it.

d). Research Invented Management Audit System Open Junior High School (SMP Terbuka) Mawar Malang Region.

Expressed of all the based data about audit that supported the school executed management increased competence teacher/tutor site III at the Open Junior High School (SMP Terbuka) Mawar Malang Region that included; (1) source; (2) message; (3) media; (4) receiver message could make front the research invented as the next;

(1) Source

    (a) Principal have said the message to the teacher/tutor.

    (b) Principal have said announcement with any way: spoken at the teacher/tutor'room, at the official, letters and meet.

    (c) Have said message the princip very fast.

(2) Message

    (a) Have said the message sometimes late and postponement.

    (b) Have said the message sometimes have not original.

    (c) Message that have said with not correction.

    (d) Have said many message that not harmony from vision and mission.

(3) Media

    (a) Media excuted through loudspeakers, blackboard, discussion, SMS although not for all, and e-mail not yet used.

    (b) Efforted media that ready for using.

    (c) Used media with approached persuasive.

    (d) At this school have used media vice as the relationship between principal with the teacher/tutor.

(4) Receiver message

    (a) Teacher/tutor have not responsibility with good.

    (b) Teacher/tutor have not noticed with good.

    (c) Teacher/tutor have not cared against information that said.

    (d) Teacher/tutor have called to discussion with teacher/tutor together at the office.

    (e) Teacher/tutor sometimes have not cared the message of the principal.

B. Analysis Trans-Site Research

1. Analysis Trans-Site I at the Open Junior High School (SMP terbuka) Teratai, Site II at (SMP Terbuka) Tulip and Site III at (SMP Terbuka) Mawar Malang Region.

a. Compared School Planned about Executed Site I at the Open Junior High School (SMP Terbuka) Teratai, Site II at (SMP Terbuka) Tulip and Site III at (SMP Terbuka) Mawar Malang region.

School Planned from dimension attitude what that must be executed at Open Junior High School (SMP Terbuka) Teratai have managerial, professional, responsibility, fair and wisdom, open, projective and unhappy with something that as routinity. This things would different with that invented at Open Junior High School (SMP Terbuka) Tulip the main from discipline attitude and consequence that have done by principal as consistence, even principal that have given sampel in a daily. Second this invented would different if have seen at the Open Juniour High School (SMP Terbuka) Mawar invented attitude that patient and sensitive.

Have seen from dimension skill to execute at the Open Junior High School (SMP Terbuka) Teratai seen more proactive, fast, strategies, happy to do the new and always at the regulation. Different invented could see at the Open Junior High School (SMP Terbuka) Tulip where principal attitude not proactive and more waited but very consistence with theirself high discipline. If compared with the both different school, thus at the Open Junior High School (SMP Terbuka) Mawar invented there are many different. Principal at this school have not ability to do the policy, but the problems the teacher/tutor have not supported principal as the leader, even have not believed with principal ability as the leader at this school.

Seen from the motivation dimension and hoped that invented at the Open Junior High School (SMP Terbuka) Teratai very high, proved that principal always "big dream," enjoy with different idea, enjoy with something that concrete, more with action than theory, optimist and projective. Others different invented at the Open Junior High School (SMP Terbuka) Tulip where principal more passive if compare with principal motivation Open Junior High School (SMP Terbuka) Teratai. But if compared both of this school with Open Junior High School (SMP Terbuka) Mawar principal only as a dreamer, but not ability to execute.

Most of the principal seen from attitude invented at the Open Junior High School (SMP Terbuka) Teratai more attitude open and "*welcome*" against whose. As at the Open Junior High School (SMP Terbuka) Tulip have a strict attitude, and consistance. As at the Open Junior High School (SMP Terbuka) Mawar have problems against patient attitude. Weakness invented at the Open Junior High School (SMP Terbuka) Teratai, principal'attitude very believed to their vice. Open Junior High School (SMP Terbuka) Tulip, principal'attitude stiff and never wanted to compromise. As at the Open Junior High School (SMP Terbuka) Mawar principal have embarrassed and sometimes said what solution problems of this school as soon as.

Unique that invented at the Open Junior High School (SMP Terbuka) Teratai principal'attitude that always wanted different with the others, Example principal have done enjoy at this school daily. For Open Junior High School (SMP Terbuka) Tulip principal'attitude have done with simple. As that invented at the Open Junior High School (SMP Terbuka) Mawar, principal that very patient against environment and community school included teacher/tutor since that made a question with this?. For more clear this image seen the table bellow.

Table 3.13. Compared School Planned about Executed Site I at the Open Juniour High School (SMP Terbuka) Teratai, Site II (SMP Terbuka) Tulip and Site III (SMP Terbuka) Mawar Malang Region.

Factor and Dimension	Quality		
	SMP T. Teratai	SMP T. Tulip	SMP T. Mawar
1. Executed attitude			
a. What that must executed	Managerial, open, scientific and professional,	Manajerial, closed, rational, stiff commitment,	Not managerial closed, rational, not commitment,

	commitment, discipline, easily substantial and fact	discipline, what there are, as rule, substantial and fact	not consistance, formality not objecktive,
b. Ability for executed	Supported benefit, proved prestation, believed and commitment	Supported benefit, proved prestation believed not total, and commitment	Not supported benefit proved prestation not believed, not consistance and not commitment
c. Motivation and desire	*"The big dreams,"* response, work with full heart and ready, but half soul for school and work with their jobs.	Response, half soul for school, and work with soul called, grace from God	less response still have contributed, not work with full heart, not work with their jobs.

b. Compared Organization Executed Site I at the Open Junior High School (SMP Terbuka) Teratai, Site II at (SMP Terbuka) Tulip and Site III at (SMP Terbuka) Mawar Malang Region.

Quality structure organization have seen from their dimension principal have done efficiency at the Open Junior High School (SMP Terbuka) Teratai, principal have done the simple jobscription, clear, respomsibility, fast, services anytime and everywhere, and efforted to be professional. Although there are the same and the different if have seen at the Open Junior High School (SMP Terbuka) Tulip, principal actually more practical, serious, and towards to the goal.if both of this school different with invented at the Open Junior High School (SMP Terbuka) Mawar would invent the fact different, principal have done jobscription although did not do and diseficiency.

Seen from dimension model that used actually if have seen at the Open Junior High School (SMP Terbuka) Teratai always used model school vision and mission,but tha's not always exactly. Different with that have done at the Open Junior High School (SMP Terbuka) Tulip, principal more focus at the model school vision and mission, teacher/tutor and at all together have done the vision and mission. If both of this school compared with Open Junior High School (SMP Terbuka) Mawar surely more contrast its different if compared with both school above, model that have but in daily practical not consistance used as model with good even sometimes have forgotten.

Dimension coordination at the Open Junior High School (SMP Terbuka) Teratai invented that principal have done jobscription and done several approached, agreement and a good corporate with the others. As for Open Junior High School (SMP Terbuka) Tulip impressed the good jobscription and responsibility. Very different with both of this school before at the Open Junior High School (SMP Terbuka) Mawar the principal have done coordination but all of done as proforma only.

Seen from benefit source power at the Open Junior High School (SMP Terbuka) Teratai most better and towards even by principal have planned as functional all of, so that they have not stiffed. This things have made to be principal for the next as formal. This things different that invented at the Open Junior High School (SMP Terbuka) Tulip, principal have used their teacher/tutor although without claimed formal only their awared, as nonformal. Different with both school above at the Open Junior High School (SMP Terbuka) Mawar could use source power at this school have not done again, they have done as awared theirself.

Most that invented at the Open Junior High School (SMP Terbuka) Teratai, principal have seen more efficient and productive for using source power. At the Open Junior High School (SMP Terbuka) Tulip teacher/tutor have awared very high, as at the Open Junior High School (SMP Terbuka) Mawar, principal'self very active.

The weakness at the Open Junior High School (SMP Terbuka) Teratai invented principal only have used the teacher/tutor, as at the Open Junior High School (SMP Terbuka) Tulip although only with their vice, different with at the Open Junior High School (SMP Terbuka) Mawar all of the teacher/tutor have not done.

Unique that invented at the Open Junior High School (SMP Terbuka) Teratai principal have desired the simple jobscription but have desired and ability at the worker, as the Open Junior High School (SMP Terbuka) Tulip principal always have helped by the vice, so that both had strong relationship. As the Open Junior High School (SMP Terbuka) Mawar all of the teacher/tutor have efforted avoid coworkers with principal and even since far from theirs. For more clear could see their imaged at this table as the next .

Table 3.14. Compared Organization Executed Site I at the Open Junior
High School (SMP Terbuka) Teratai, Site II at (SMP Terbuka) Tulip
and Site III at (SMP Terbuka) Mawar Malang Region.

Factor and Dimension	Qualiaty		
	SMP T. Teratai	SMP T. Tulip	SMP T. Mawar
2. Structure Organization			
a. Efficiency	Simply, Organization,	Simply, Organization,	Simply, Organization,

	Jobscription, Respon sibility, procedural, and discipline.	Jobscription, Respon sibility, procedure, And discipline.	Jobscription, Respon sibility, not procedu ral, and not executed.
b. Model	At the school vision and mission as creati ve	At the school vision and misi as absolute	At the school vision and mission but not consistance
c. Coordination	Coordinate as regular with responsibility	Coordinate as regular with responsibility	Coordinate but not responsibility
d. Benefit source power	Functional, Integrated, Responsiblity Discipline, Build,	Integrated, responsibility, disciupline, not build	Integrated but not full responsibility, not discipline, not build

C. Compared Development Source Power Management Executed Site I at the Open Junior High School (SMP Terbuka) Teratai, Site II at (SMP Terbuka) Tulip and Site III at (SMP Terbuka) Mawar Malang Region.

Quality source power have seen from dimension teacher/tutor and principal at the Open Junior High School (SMP Terbuka) Teratai have seen from factor source power teacher/tutor as quantity still less, proved still there are teacher/tutor that ass honorer. As quality still there are teacher/tutor have not graduated (S1), teacher/tutor that taught trans skill, still many teacher/tutor not yet past certification examination and commonly teacher/tutor weak at the imformatica technology (IT) or have not learnt. Same with at the Open Junior High School (SMP Terbuka) Tulip even worse, there are teacher/tutor have pension that used to teach again, sometimes happen changed teacher/tutor at the several time and resign. In and out teacher/tutor depended with their commitment between teacher/tutor with institution, that's ability the teacher/tutor could adaptation with the rule of the school. From both of this school would see different at the Open Junior High School (SMP Terbuka) Mawar covered less of the teacher/tutor of this school that have taught double lessons like religion and language, so that practical learning quality worse. Teacher/tutor that only at their lessos as their skill at this school.

Seen from dimension facility build physic and instrument at the Open Junior High School (SMP Terbuka) Teratai as quantity have seen complete and variation, from school building, class and infrastructure learning and the others like multy-media room, internet, laboratorium, library, sport infrastructure and development-self have prepared and very supported against executed school policy, even till now still done to build. As quality all infrastructure already for using and free for school procedur using with responsibility, so that as development informatica technology instrument learning that have at this school specification up to date, only weak from used and maintance the instrument and their budget have not used

There are different with Open Junior High School (SMP Terbuka) Tulip that all facility physic built and instrument complete, but they have planned with good the building, infrastructure, so that have prepared the budget for maintancing and anticipation for the future. Principle managed they was that priority, rational at the needed. So that all facility physic have representative, good proportional and professional from how to order and maintance with planned and a good cared, that's reality effective and efficient.

Different both of this school would see more different at the Open Junior High School (SMP Terbuka) Mawar actually they have facility and instrument that same with both of the school, but this school weak from management like from planned system, so that influence against executed, control and evaluation, that last impact to the principal as the leader. Invented many learning instrument that have not completed, for saving have not placed at the place and many the condition have damaged and have not used again.

Seen from the dimension source fund at the Open Junior High School (SMP Terbuka) Teratai have source financial that routine as the budget and financial from Government centre and region, but at the others side this school have found from "*generating income*" from culinary and dress activity that have done from this school and the fact many sponsor that have helped because have done to coorperate with this school although this event only tentative. So that as quantity their fund more and health if seen from "*cash flow*" financial.

As different with site at the Open Junior High School (SMP Terbuka) Tulip and source fund at this school closed, financial this school as the institution responsibility, although actually principal couls know from school treasure. So that if someone asked how much budget institution and from where the funded, principal have not known. If principal have neded something thus made proposal to institution. Institution would consider and agree. During this principal felt from financial still normal, fluent and have never problem ready all for this school. As quantity and quality they have the budget and still health.

Both site at this school would see different if seen at the Open Junior High School (SMP Terbuka) Mawar, source financial this school as administrative same source at the budget at this school would see different at the Open Junior High School (SMP Terbuka Mawar), source financial at this school as administrative same source at the budget and routine financial and financial from government centre or region, or from sponsor that tentative. But at the executed budget that have at the budget sometimes have not used as the planned, since the treasure sometimes have not money more. Even sometimes have invented buying something out of the budget, as that have budgeted not priority. Impression principal with the teacher/tutor have cared and controlled each others, and used the budget very fast who's the first that founded. So that as quantity and quality financial of this school not health in its condition that"*cash flow*".

If have seen at the third school, the fact invented there are equal that have pulled as the conclusion that this third school have source routine financial based at the each budget and several funed from government centre and region, also funded tentative from financial others that used to execute the policy school. This third school have budgeted, although the fact at the executed different one others that impact at their condition financial.

Different condition source financial at the Open Junior High School (SMP Terbuka) Teratai used more orientation at the real desire when have desired, desired as the moment, irregular financial administration without seen the priority, and that crucial finished at that time, how the next princip. At last financial would be damaged and in confised not "*on priority*" again. As at the Open Junior High School (SMP Terbuka) Teratai institution managed the financial with the priority and rational/concrete management, considered to use level professional, their princip wanted effective and efficient for the next institution. As at the Open Junior High School (SMP Terbuka) Tulip mopre towards at the managed financial irregular, who the first used financial that's integrated to be found, but who late used the financial have used the others. Thus sometimes event school have not financial.

The most that invented from each school, at the Open High School (SMP Terbuka) Teratai problem source financial open who's could give input as free about financial; discipline the noted as the invoice; and school consequence responsibility each fund that used. Different with at the Open Junior High School (SMP Terbuka) Tulip each budget safe financial, clear and objective so that avoided from deviation because have used the priority budget and consequence institution also with function and as there are. As the Open Junior High School (SMP Terbuka) Mawar each teacher/tutor as the controlled a good financial.

The weakness invented at the Open Junior High School (SMP Terbuka) Teratai financial school confused, when the financial that used for school desired, thus would be free and heavy responsibility, the solution must seeked for alternative others financial more, and the last created cycle that no the end. For the Open Junior High School (SMP Terbuka) Tulip the principal weakness not creative and not the test skill leader from one side about managed financial that must expert, so that principal never have done about managed financial, even desired to ask the skill principal about management school financial. At the Open Junior High School (SMP Terbuka) Mawar invented this school weakness never advanced as that real; teacher/tutor have not used "*sense of belonging*" that respomsibility, so that desired at the moment and for the future "*up graded*" again the management.

Unique that invented at the Open Junior High School (SMP Terbuka) Teratai seen from dimension source financial more health, but at the practical still also less budget financial. As the Open Junior High School (SMP Terbuka) Tulip with financial only there are at the institution and never less budget. As at the Open Junior High School (SMP Terbuka) Mawar source school financial always less budget and not as with princip management in managing school financial. But this third school queer still could do at the Malang region. For more clear imaged seen from table as this below.

Table 3.15 Compared Development Source Power Management Executed Site I at the Open Junior High School (SMP Terbuka) Teratai, Site II at (SMP Terbuka) Tulip and Site III at (SMP Terbuka) Mawar Malang Region.

Factor and Dimension	Quality		
	SMP T. Teratai	SMP T. Tulip	SMP T. Mawar
3. Source power			
a. Human	As quantity still less and quality enough good.	As quantity sill less and as quality enough good.	As quantity still less and as quality enough good
b. Physic/ facility and instrument	As quantity enough complete, and as quality have not used as optimal impression not cared.	As quantity enough complete, and as quality have not used as optimal impression not cared.	As quantity enough complete, and as quality have used as optimal impression not cared.
c. Financial	As good quantity, budget from govern ment, *"generating income"* as quality and *"cash flow"* health financial as the budget.	As good quantity, budget fro govern ment, manged institu tion as closed, and *"cash flow"* health financial, as procedu re, fact desired at the scala priority	As good quantity, budget from govern ment, and as quality *"cash flow."* financial not health because not discipline, not clear, the used and someti me fictive out of budget.

d. Compared Management Audit System Site I at the Open Junior High School (SMP Terbuka) Teratai, Site II at (SMP Terbuka) Tulip and Site III at (SMP Terbuka) Mawar Malang Region.

Quality audit management principal have seen from dimension at the Open Junior High School (SMP Terbuka) Teratai have comunikative, reference and objective and orginil also experience at the policy communication. Different with Open Junior High School (SMP Terbuka) Tulip if have seen from level communication experiencestill less. As the Open Junior High School (SMP Terbuka) Mawar if compared with both others school very different as significant I all aspect communication. Have seen not distinct and not able convince also level experience, have not a long experience school leader. So that if have seen from the leader still must be learnt many and made experience.

Seen from dimension message the Open Junior High School (SMP Terbuka) Teratai always efforted to find information that *"up to date,"* fast and orginal. Message that have said with clear and fix. The message always come to school vision and mission. This things invented also at the Open Junior High School (SMP Terbuka) Tulip that notabene the managed institution, so that message that have said as soon as, clear, transparent and could responsibility. Others things at the Open Junior High School (SMP Terbuka) Mawar principal have not abled because there are not teacher/tutor that supported, they are not active asked, and seeked for all self information the new one. Message that have not said factual, not transparent and not could responsibility. Beside that communication that have said not objektive, not distinct, worry,not representative and not considered as accurate, so have not clear commitment.

Seen from dimension media, many aspect that could describe between others; source power human (teacher/tutor), facility infrastructure and financial. At the Open Junior High School (SMP terbuka) Teratai, as quantity or quality still less, so that sustainanble of the teacher/tutor for the future at this school what could overthere. Commonly teacher/tutor not professional still worked as the routine limited, formality and monoton, even actually they are not decent to teach, what else for school standard international. Facility/infrastructure that have prepared expression have not used and effective even at the building without a good planned. As financial although many source but still less and to much financial out of the budget. This things have done at the Open Junior High School (SMP Terbuka) Tulip, seen from aspect source power human (teacher/ tutor), have not the quality and quantity. This things have seen at the honorary teacher/tutor and pension that still have used and teacher/tutor qualification still low from that standard. Facility that have prepared enough but if have not seen from the benefit optimal because afraid damaged. The condition that have done more made stiff at the Open Junior High School (SMP Terbuka) Mawar, the teacher/tutor have not wanted to learn Informatica Technology and have felt decent to use facility that have prepared at the school and considered still not yet to learn. Infrastructure facility at this school have prepared but have not used as optimal even impression have not cared.

Seen from dimension received message at the Open Junior High School (SMP Terbuka) Teratai still there are between teacher/tutor have known the principal'need, message have not all of known as throughly of theirs, each teacher/tutor have done the vision and mission. As the Open Junior high School (SMP Terbuka) Tulip, have said the principal message and could receive thoroughly by the teacher/tutor, although when executed the policy they felt forced even more impression as the instructive because all the policy from institution. Condition that very ugly happened at the Open Junior High School (SMP Terbuka) Mawar, received aspect message at this school have not supported the policy implementation. This things happened principal and teacher/tutor'relationship have not harmony, so that the message have not received with good by the teacher/tutor. This things principal and teacher/tutor'relationship have done without the school vision and mission, only teacher/tutor still have felt response against the school, except for the young teacher/tutor.

If phenomena at the Open Junior High School (SMP Terbuka) Teratai, (SMP Terbuka) Tulip and (SMP Terbuka) Mawar have conclusive invented at the third equality principal efforted a good policy communication to their teacher/tutor as each their policy that have said could execute as the school vision and mission. The based different that could see at principal styles communication, at the Open Junior High School (SMP Terbuka) Teratai more enterprener bureaucrary style, as (SMP Terbuka) Tulip most bureaucrary style, as (SMP Terbuka) Mawar more politic bureaucrary style.

From different communication style this things most invented at the Open Junior High School (SMP Terbuka) Teratai communication that have said with full hoped (optimist), projective, hot and concrete; always creative, innovative, even different with others; and each the information could responsibility. For (SMP Terbuka) Tulip communication that have said with clear and objektive, to the point, and consider with fast. As (SMP Terbuka) Mawar could be fair, awareness and free communication. Although from the different style invented less each others, at (SMP Terbuka) Teratai with communication that open sometimes the message to be not clear because appeared any version known as each other; sometimes have needed a long time; and could lose value communication. At (SMP Terbuka) Tulip communication more closely, stiff, stress, arrogant and instructive. As at (SMP Terbuka) Mawar communication more not clear, and only have hoped self-awareness, created communication that hypocrite, slander and made broken into pieces; even the communication have deviated from vision and mission that have been hoped because that appear communication individual that's very urgent.

Although unique from each thid school have seen from dimension communication at (SMP Terbuka) Teratai open communication (*multy ways traffic communication*); at (SMP Terbuka) Tulip stiff communication (*one way traffic communication*) and closed even "*no comment.*" As at (SMP Terbuka) Mawar flurry communication (*crawded traffic communication*) and have not believed one to the others. Although at the daily fact this third school have high believeness at the community as the excellent school that always very interested at their environment, proved have seen at the many documentation prestation rewards. So that made clear the imaged could see from table as the next.

Table 3.16. Compared Management Audit System Site I at the Open Junior High School (SMP Terbuka) Teratai, Site II at (SMP Terbuka) Tulip and Site III at (SMP Terbuka) Mawar Malang Region.

Factor and Dimension	Qualitas		
	SMP.T.Teratai	SMP.T.Tulip	SMP.T. Mawar
4. Audit			
a. Source	Expert, experience commitment, panctual, quality believed,	Not experience depend on, closed, commitment, panctual, quality,	Enough Expert, not yet experience not commitment, not believed,
b. Message	Objective, orginal, warm and interested	Objektive, orginal, not warm and not interested,	Sometimes objective, post pone.
c. Media	Good and representative	Good and representative	Good and not representative
d. Received message	Response, received with good discuss and done	Response, received with good discuss and done	Not response, make'question, did not do.

2. Analysis Trans-Site I at the Open Junior High School (SMP terbuka) Teratai, Site II at (SMP Terbuka) Tulip and Site III at (SMP Terbuka) Mawar Malang Region.

a. Compared School Planned about Executed that Managed Site I at the Open Junior High School (SMP Terbuka) Teratai, Site II at (SMP Terbuka) Tulip and Site III at (SMP Terbuka) Mawar Malang Region.

Quality planned school have seen from attitude dimension what that must managed by principal at (SMP Terbuka) Teratai liked commonly attitude managerial have efforted with good. if have seen from aspect ability principal managed could responsibility even principal have leader commitment and motivation that high managed this school. Different with principal attitude at (SMP Terbuka) Tulip if have seen from aspect principal ability was low, because the principal could not do something at this school and limited by institutions so that impact at the level their motivation. If both of this school compared with at (SMP Terbuka) Mawar thus would invent that more ugly, thid different seen at the same aspect with (SMP Terbuka) Tulip that principal'ability have done their as the leader of this school low, because principal have not supported the teacher/tutor. Principal'efforted have done approached formal and nonformal. For more clear the imaged could see at the table as the next.

Table 3.17. Compared School Planned about Executed that have Managed Site I at the Open Junior High School (SMP Terbuka) Teratai, Site II at (SMP Terbuka) Tulip and Site III at (SMP Terbuka) Mawar Malang Region..

Factor and Dimension	Quality		
	SMP T. Teratai	SMP T. Tulip	SMP T. Mawar
1. Executed Attitude			
a. What that must done	Supported and guide, towards, look for alternative, done as professional.	Supported and change, asked, facility, done as rational, asked.	Not supported, not help, not changed, not asked, facility and done as rational and irrational.
b. Ability for managing	Supported, emphasized, fact prestation, believed, distinct and with clear sanction.	Supported, emphasized, proved fact prestation, believed, Distinct, with clear sanction.	Not supported, not sanction, proved with fact prestation, and believed, not distinct.
c. Motivation and desired	Responsibility, *"The big dreams,"* work with intentions and victimized.	Responsibility, and victimized, work with soul called, grace from the God.	Not responsibility and victimized, work with intentions but difficult at the practical.

b. Compared Organization Executed that Managed Site I at the Open Junior High School (SMP Terbuka) Teratai, Site II at (SMP Terbuka) Tulip and Site III at (SMP Terbuka) Mawar Malang Region.

Quality structure organization have seen from dimension efficiency that principal have done at the Open Junior High School (SMP Terbuka) Teratai, simple and not trouble and principal efforted with good.

Seen from dimension model that have used as school vision and mission. For coordination dimension have professional and proportional, seen from dimension used source power with their skill as optimal. This fact things have equality with principal have done at the Open Junior High School (SMP Terbuka) Tulip. But if the invented of the both school different with at (SMP Terbuka) Mawar have not executed and all seem bad although have efforted, because teacher/

tutor have apathetic. Principal have hard efforted to do with approached formal and nonformal. For more clear could see the imaged at the table as the next.

Table 3.18. Compared Organization Executed that Managed Site I at the Open Junior High School (SMP Terbuka) Teratai, Site II at (SMP Terbuka) Tulip and Site III at (SMP Terbuka) Mawar Malang Region.

Factor and Dimension	Quality		
	SMP T. Teratai	SMP T. Tulip	SMP T. Mawar
2. Structure Organization			
a. Efficiency	Jobscription with clear, responsibility, simpily, organization, as procedure.	Jobscription with clear, responsibility, simpily, organization, As procedure,	Jobscription with clear, responsibility, simpily, organization, as procedure but not supported.
b. Model	At the school vision and mission, pledge as the rule, discipline, sanction.	At the school vision and mission, pledge as the rule, discipline, heavy sanction	At the school vision and mission, pledge as the rule, not discipline, sanction not clear.
c. Coordination	Done the rule, distinct, coordinate, always given easily and believeness, responsibility.	Done the rule, distinct, coordinate, always given believe ness and responsibility.	Done the rule, not execution because without supported from teacher/tutor
d. Benefit source power	Functional, integrated responsibility, discipline.	Functional, responsi bility, discipline.	Have Planned but not execution because teacher/tutor not supported.

c. Compared Development Source Power Management Executed that Managed Site I at the Open Junior Hugh School (SMP Terbuka) Teratai, Site II at (SMP Terbuka) Tulip and Site III at (SMP Terbuka) Mawar Malang Region.

Quality development source power have seen from dimension at the Open Junior High School (SMP Terbuka) Teratai for aspect teacher/tutor, facility physic and instrument, source financial as quantity or quality principal have efforted. Even if have seen from sustainable this school develop and better for the future. Invented the same things at (SMP Terbuka) Tulip. Although if both of this school compared with (SMP Terbuka) Mawar seen very different from source power human and weak at the source financial. This things principal have not abled to build this school with good, although have efforted to do with any approached objective that formal or nonformal. For more clear the imaged could see from table as the next.

Table 3.19 Compared Development Source Power Management Executed that Managed Site I at the Open Junior High School (SMP Terbuka) Teratai, Site II at (SMP Terbuka) Tulip and Site III at (SMP Terbuka) Mawar Malang Region.

Factor and Dimension	Quality		
	SMP T. Teratai	SMP T.Tulip	SMP T. Mawar
3. Source power			
a. Human	Take up that honorary teacher/tutor, made seat of the teacher/tutor at their room, changed invoice pack age book.	Take up that honorary teacher/tutor, made seat of the teacher/Tutor at their room, changed invoice pack book, permit for learning, have pension.	Take up that honorary teacher/tutor, made seat of the teacher/tutor at their room, changed invoice package book, permit for learning.
b. Physic/ facility and instrument	Added, maintenance, cared, with procedu cer, responsibility, distinct sanction.	Repaired, maintanan ce, cared, with proce ducer, responsibility.	Repaired, not maintanance not cared, not procedurer without sanction.
c. Financial	At the budget, collec ted the fund Govern ment, managed *"generating income"* looking for	At the budget, closed proved with invoiced, discipline, with proce dure, and at the fact desire, and priority	At the budget, closed, tertutup, not discipline, not consistance, with fact desire and priority.

"*sponsorship*" proved scale.
With "*invoice,*" dis
cipline, priority scale,
at the fact desire.

---

d. Compared Management Audit Syatem that managed Site I at the Open Junior High School (SMP Terbuka) Teratai, Site II at (SMP Terbuka) Tulip and Site III at (SMP Terbuka) Mawar Malang Region.

Quality management audit system that principal have done at the Open Junior High School (SMP Terbuka) Teratai have seen from good dimension source for aspect renew, transformational, clarity, accurate, and consistency so that principal efforted with good. This things different with that efforted at the Open Junior High School (SMP Terbuka) Tulip for aspect received message, teacher/tutor have received the message impression instructive. Different both of this school would more clear again if compared with invented at (SMP Terbuka) Mawar, seen from aspekct have not accurated, aspect media noti representative and aspect received message where teacher/tutor have believed and still worry with the message that have found. This things principal and teacher/tutor relationship was worse, but principal have efforted to do with any approached formal and nonformal. For more clear about the imaged could see at the table as the next.

Table 3.20. Compared Management Audit System that Managed Site I at the Open Junior High School (SMP Terbuka) Teratai, Site II at (SMP Terbuka) Tulip and Site III at (SMP Terbuka) Mawar Malang Region.

Factor and Dimension	Quality		
	SMP.T.Teratai	SMP.T.Tulip	SMP.T. Mawar
4. Audit			
a. Source	Principal said, with meeting, announcement, insignia of office, what there are.	Principal said, with meeting, announcement, insignia of office, What there are.	Principal said, with meeting, announcement, insignia of office, As the urgent.
b. Message	Have said as soon as, source clear fact, accurate, not deviate from.	Have said as soon as, source clear fact, accurate, not deviate from.	Have said as soon as, source clear fact, accurate, not deviate from.

c. Media	Done from loud speaker, blackboard, discuss, meeting, and SMS.	Done from speaker, blackboard, discuss, meeting.	Done from loud speaker, blackboard, discuss, meeting, SMS, and mouth to mouth.
d. Received message	Response, seek for information, discussion.	Response, seek for information, discussion.	Not response, not information, without discussion, even ridicule.

C. Research Invented between Site and Proposition at Management Activity Open Junior High School (SMP Terbuka).

Result analysis multi-sites, the research invented between site and proposition school management activity, were (1) research invented between site and drafted proporsition planned school about management Open Junior High School; (2) research invented site and drafted proporsition management organization at the Open Junior High School; (3) research invented between site and drafted proporsition development power source at the management Open Junior High School; and (4) research invented between site and drafted proporsition system audit management at the Open Junior High School.

1). Research Invented between Site and Proposition Planned School at the Open Junior High School.

(a) The Planing of the school, principal have done any policy for increasing competence of the teacher at the school, although have weakness at effort the management shool was the principal style that did not known the condition of the school so the management as unconcern.

(b) The principal potency, most of the management school could not done excellent. Because most obstacle than factor to support it. Obstacle from very low the humanity quality, so uncreative. Each management only for this time, if have a new one that could not used it.

(c) Principal motivation and desire for adavancing the school must a good supported from another, but principal attitude that proactive and projection. The good management, factual and all of known about it. Optimal socialization before done the management.

Scheme comunication management with dimension as figure 3.1. shown as the next:

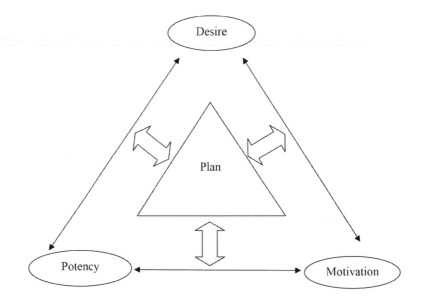

Figure 3.1. Planned School about Management at Open Junior High School

1) Proposition Research about Management School Planning at The Open Junior High School

P1.1 Teacher attitude against management planned manajemen confirm by school climate, succeed and easi relation one to another with full surrender.

P1.2 If the teacher have desired, potency and high commitment from principal attitude, therefore school management planning effectively.

P1.3 If principal could used their vice, then principal have done its good job 75%.

P1.4 If Jika discipline and responsible could done with full knowledge, then the school management have done 60%.

P1.5 Every principal have unique attitude managed it school, then school have a actual imaged and interested at the management school.

2) Research Invented betweet Site and Management Proposition organization at Open Junior High School.

(a) Organization structure the efficiency organization school imaged, good or not. It have seen between its organization school. If organization structure at another, it was depended at the each Characteristic school, there are school the result have done the opened character. There are school the result have done closed character, and there are no ascertain character.

(b) The good organization structure if its managed always at the clear standard visi misi school, then its result would at its structure. But if have done far from the standard visi misi, then its result would not clear and no towards.

(c) The urgent coordination at the management school have a clear job description and responsible. With the good job description occoured the good coordination, so that have the towards responsible and this school coordination was the urgent for it.

(d) Benefit power source as the urgent part at the management school, it was usual as function at the all jobs to vice principal and the teacher so that could have a good discipline and responsible.

So that the school with its dimension could seen at figure 3.2. as the next.

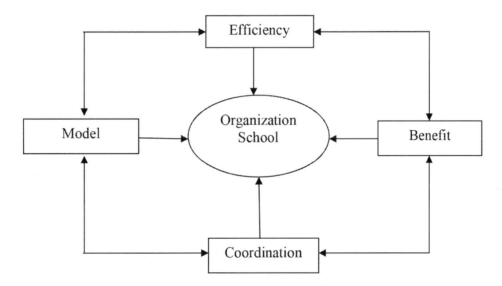

Figure 3.2. Management organization at the Open Junior High School.

2) Research Proposition about Management Organization at The Open Junior High School

P2.1 If organization have done good, since not appear unhappy and bad.

P2.2 The good organization structure would be supported all of continue with clear organization.

P2.3 If the good organization structure continuing and sipporting with done effective, efficiency, the clear Model, the good coordination and everybody done it, since the school would be succeed.

3) Research invented between Site and Development Proposition Management Power Source at the Open Junior High School.

(a) Quantity of the school still deceased teacher, since principal used honor teacher as with its need. But the quality teacher could not teached in the class, even still many teacher could not used the technology in other jog. Since the school could be imaged with power source like that, the teacher could supported the effective management school.

(b) The weakness of teacher at school, their english language, computer, access internet, even its knowledge undevelop because the teacher still in conventional. How could supported the effective implementation and a good management school.

(c) Physical facility and instrument at the school, only as useful not yet optimal and have no maintenance. So the facility instrument was no useful, even for another school have no maintenance. Because have no budget for maintenance and always was forgotten at its budgeting, so that the scholl could not payed the labor and technician. During quality, facility instrument at the school available, still good, only decreased its maintenance and damaged.

(d) From source of the budget for costing of the school was enough, but weak at managed the funding. Because attitude management have not discipline with using the money, many payment have not with the budget, that not at the field as the needed, and have not used to the priority scale that have a real budget. Principal still have a high speculation mental, without the right thought, and the final borrow funding. Funding, implementation management school have not optimal by the principal, because pay attention at the physical change school. How clear design integrated audit management school with its dimension see figure 3.3 as the next;

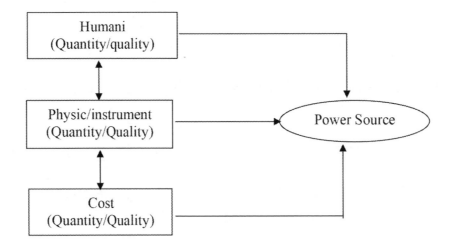

Figure 3.3. Development Managemant Power Source at The Open Junior High School

3) Research Proposition about Development Management Power Source at the Open Junior High School.

P3.1 If humanity source at the school about quantity and quality have balanced, even acceleration occurred at the succeed management activity school.

P3.2 Facility instrument have prepared at the school would impact positive against progressive technology that could build self confidence of the teacher at the school, but the quality would impact against formed crisis level, creativity and innovative at the management school.

P3.3 If the good budget have supported the management school, so that the education would be more progressive and a good character.

P3.4 If power source have prepared at the school, the teacher could used all of with optimal, principal and student would have a good quality against management school.

P3.5 Quality management school would done excellent, if have supported with al the stakeholder at the school.

4). Research Invented between Site and Proposition System Audit Management at the Open Junior High School.

(a) Management school have supported the principal at the audit management that would said to the teacher at the school. Principal managed the school in communication as source that audit the management, so that could be excellent, qualiy, effective and professional.

(b) Principal have done the management school with skill of the principal used systematic communication, with action body intonation that given a good self-confidence to their teacher as the getting message.

(c) Communication that principal have said to be known, if the communication have supported by objective source message, even created the urgent communication.

(d) Communication that experience principal, religiously, excellent as the leader, all the message have said more self-confidence of the teacher. Very different if as asually communication of the principal.

(e) The context message content that the principal have said in audit management school to the teacher with effective, quality and professional if the message up to date, transformational, clear, valid and unchanged or consistent so could be responsible.

(f) For the new message management have said as the right message to the teacher not the old message, so the teacher wanted to know that message.

(g) Transformational that message have said as the actually fact occured to the community and needed to know with good. The message'content needed actually fact to the teacher, not only for a special group.

(h) The clearness message even each message of management that principal have said would effective if the message could be received with good to the teacher done management school, so the objective actually message.

(i) The message would be efective and quality if in the principal comunication message have said with accurately, right and as the observation, discussion and with the high commitment, so that the message more in the self-confidence.

(j) Besides, principal have done the message with audit would given effect against the teacher if have said not consistent, always change and uncertain. If principal have said the message not change as the content and purpose the teacher could be effective and done its all the message. All the order not far from the aim, visi, misi, that could done to everyone at the school.

(k) Principal have audited with more believed the actually fact, if its communication have supported with any message could be received and very representative to give the mean against the message that have done in audit management so that could known by the teacher with good.

(l) Principal' message audit management school have done for its teacher have received with good, the weakness of the style principal said unconditional that deceased self-confidence our teacher to receive the message. So many effects the audit message could be received with good. How integrated communication management school with dimension see figure 3.4. as the next;

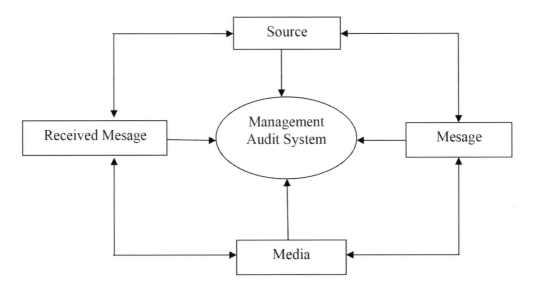

Figure 3.4. Management Audit System at the Open Junior High School.

4) Research Proposition about Management Audit System at the Open Junior High School.

P4.1 If principal with management audit system around the school socialization and good, so that management implementation school could be effective and excellent.

P4.2 The effective management audit school would created if supported the source information could be responsible, although from expert information, reference that supported the information, although the accurate righteousness level could believed credibility level.

P4.3 If principal at the management communication school could done with good, would created the teacher'confidence as an excellent receiver.

P4.4 School management audit that effective would created supported message, from fact, clear, up to date with as the visi, misi, that be hoped.

P4.5 School management audit that effective would created to support as much as message used, made easy to said that information and representative the actually message.

P4.6 School management audit that efective would created to receive message infrastructure as the clear source comunication.

P4.7 School management audit that efective if source supported could responsible all the information have said, with the clear message, and for the believed receiver and representative.

Invented formulation at three Sites were: at SMP Terbuka Teratai, SMP Terbuka Tulip and SMP Terbuka Mawar at the Malang Region.

Table 3.21. Invented Formulation School Planned about Management have done at Site I SMP Terbuka Teratai, Site II di SMP Terbuka Tulip and Site III SMP Terbuka Mawar at Malang Region.

Dimension	Site I	Site II	Site III	Invent
1. Managed Attitude				
a. What must be done	Support, Build, towards, facility, look for alternative, done, professional	Support, Helping, change, ask, facility done, done rational	not support, helping, change, ask. facility, done, rational and irrational	Management activity have done by Principal at three sites as the source

b. Ability to do	Support, Emphasize, Prestige, Believed, distinct and doubt.	Support Emphasize prestige believed, distinct doubt.	not support no doubt have prestige believed, no distinct No doubt	pointed that between one site with another have ability, that same motivation,
c. Motivation and desire	Responsible, Job, Sincere	Responsible, Job, Sincere	not responsible Sincere	only emphasize to each different site

Table 3.22. Invented formulation Management Organization have done at Site I SMP Terbuka Teratai, Site II SMP Terbuka Tulip, and Site III SMP Terbuka Mawar at the Malang Region.

Dimensi	Site I	Site II	Site III	Temuan
2. Structure Organization				
a. Efficiency Distinct,	Job distinct, responsible organization, procedure	Job distinct, responsible organization, procedure,	Job distinct responsible organization, not procedure,	Principal done activity at three sites efficiency as planning, coordination,
b. Model	Visi, Misi discipline, doubt	Visi, Misi, discipline, doubt	Visi, Misi discipline, no doubt	used the same power source only emphasize
c. Coordination	Used the role, discipline, distinct, coordination, easily, believing, responsible,	used the role, discipline, distinct, coordination, believing, responsible	not used the role, not support from the teacher	to each site different with the school'need

d. Useful power source	Function, responsible discipline	Function, responsible discipline	Planning no action no supported from the teacher.

Table 3.23 Development Invented Formulation Management Power Source that have done at Site I SMP Terbuka Teratai, Site II SMP Terbuka Tulip, and Site III SMP Terbuka Mawar at the Malang Region.

Dimension	Site I	Site II	Site III	Invented
3. Power Source				
a. Humanity	Received teacher, academic akademik prepared for teacher, book changing learning permit,	Received teacher, academic akademik prepared for teacher book changing, learning permit,	Received teacher, academic akademik prepared for teacher book changing, as school needed	Humanity power source activity at three sites could prepared the instrument facility, maintenance, and funding, as the same criteria, only each different site
b. Physic/ facility and instrument	Increased, prepared, maintenance, procedure responsible doubt, distinct,	Repaired, maintenance, procedure responsible	Prepared, Repaired, unguarded, maintenance, procedure not doubt, distinct,	
c. Funding	Budget finding sponsorship Billing Discipline, The fact Needed Procedure Priority scale,	Budget closely proved billing discipline, procedure, the fact needed priority scale	Budget not discipline, not consisten, tidak komsisten with demand, the fact needed priority scale	

Table 3.24. Invented Formulation Management Audit System Audit that
have done at Site I SMP Terbuka Teratai, Site II SMP Terbuka Tulip,
and Site III SMP Terbuka Mawar at the Malang Region.

Dimension	Site I	Site II	Site III.	Temuan.
4. Audit				
a. Source,	Principal said, used anykind at the meeting, announcement at official,	Principal said, used anykind kepala sekolah, announcement at official,	Principal said, usedanykind kepala sekolah, announcement at official	Have done at the three sites message could pointed as the activity and certain criteria management
b. Message	Said as soon as, the fact distinct source, as the message,	said as soon as, the fact distinct source, as the message, sometimes late,	said as soon as, the fact distinct source, as the message, sometimes late,	processing. The same management learning but principal, teacher each site covered with its job style.
c. Media	From loud speaker, white board, discussion, meeting, SMS.	From loud speaker, white board, discussion, meeting	From loud speaker, white board, discussion, meeting, SMS,	
d. Received message	Respond, looking for other information, discussion.	Respond, looking for other information discussion.	Unresponsive, no other information, pay attention, no discussion	

CHAPTER IV

Discussion

At the chapter before have done data and research invented to each sites also analysis between site to ascertain the final research invented. In this chapter to explain the discussion about research invented from of the three sites research with empirical analysis and theory. This invented discussion included at the aim that result from whole focus research, were: the school management condition have done at 1. SMP Terbuka Teratai; 2. SMP Terbuka Tulip; and 3. SMP Terbuka Mawar at the Malang region.

1. Planned about Management at the Open Junior High School (SMP Terbuka) Teratai, Tulip and Mawar at the Malang Region

Planned about management at SMP Terbuka Teratai Malang region, were; management attitude factor could seen from principal management dimension that supported, made the community known each management school, example principal effort to support the teacher to follow certification, given funding to the teacher were wanted to learn and changed all of the books where bought with bill, till asked the teacher have done management difficulty. Principal effort have done many with consent, like to return the money where have bought for the school.

Ability Principal dimension done school management ability have many occur changed basic, each management that have done always found teacher supporting and because a good management, useful and proven, mainly integrated with teacher competence problem at this school, indicasion could seen from prestige that from the school, community confidence against the school, and result of the student examination. Principal'concept, operasional and ability social relation integrated, could seen the prove.

Motivation dimension and desire, principal have done and responsible against the school, message with confidence sometimes everyone to curl, come early and back home lately, always worked at the school, active bought and read selt-motivation book, leadership and religious. Principal used its motorcycle, but always enjoy with their job. Everywhere to be principal could advanced that school, only with their discipline. (Tilaar, 1997:151) obtained "education have a function to teach each citizen, prepared power that have characteristic that desire for industrial, but not as that main responsible".

If all this phenomenal as proposition even surely that principal was a management that understood about task and responsible as the primcipal, ability a good management and have leadership material and experience as the leadership because have as a principal around 15 years, so that expert as the leadership. Finally that management attitude quality principal against management school have effort with the good till supported management at this school. The principal managed not formal because their very familiar.

Planned about management SMP Terbuka Tulip at the Malang Region, were; attitude factor management seen from dimension what must principal management was supported, given to the teacher to follow certification, funding for the teacher that wanted to learn and changed the money what books lesson have bought as the bill, till what difficulty of the teacher at the management school.

Principal ability dimension management school have many changed from the basic, each management always found supported from the teacher and result from the good management, useful and proven, integrated with teacher competence problem at this school, indicasion could seen from prestige that the school, community confidence against schdol and exanmination result student. Concept principal, operasional and social relationship have done good.

Principal motivation dimension, desire, and responsible against the school, always early come and than back home lately from the school, school to be a second home and religiously. Principal went to school with walking, never give up. Principal believed that motivation and discipline as the key for succeeding of the school.

If all this phenomena with accurate as proposition certainly that principal was a management that understood the task and responsible, have ability and a high motivation a good management. Finally the principal management attitude quality against management school have effort with good till supported management at this school and all as a formal

Planned about management at SMP Terbuka Mawar at the Malang Region, were; attitude factor have seen from management principal before supported, helped and seek way out alternative, at each management school, example principal efforted the teacher to follow certification, funding to the teacher that wanted to learn and changed the money books as the bill, till asked the difficulty of the teacher before done management. If also have done never not professional.

Principal ability dimension done management school the event have not changed, each management that have not supported from the teacher and its result unproved, the first integrated with competence problem teacher at this school.

Motivation dimension and desire, were principal have not managed and full responsible against the school, no message with confidence that have been given, sometimes principal early come and than fast back home, enjoy reading self-motivation book, leadership and religious and liked to say the difficulty.

If all this phenomena accurate as proposition could certainly that principal was not managerial that understood the task and responsible as principal, have not ability a good management, high motivation, responsible. Principal have experience to lead the school below 10 years, so have not seen as the leadership. Finally certainly that disposition quality and attitude principal against management school have been efforted but not yet good and supported at this school. Principal have done the management school with uncertain.

2. Management Organization at the Open Junior High School (SMP Terbuka) Teratai, Tulip and Mawar at the Malang Region.

Management organization SMP Terbuka Teratai at Malang Region with organization structure factor that principal have done for efficiency dimension was the clear job description with vice, vice have functional at their task with given confidence and full responsible, done the discipline and prosedure with clear job description have done vice and all the teacher, treasurer and administration as with their each ability. Principal always done at the school visi, misi as the model so that did what the real role, used the discipline, as the "*softcopy*" and "*hardcopy*" data file, noted and booked, bill proved and with excellent reported. Seek all the file with easily and kept with accurately, proved at this school. Principal ccordination dimension with given responsible, confidential, task totheir vice, teacher/tutor, treasurer and administration with purpose to make the coordination easily and done step by step. This thing impact at the useful good and exactly power source.

From the all phenomena would be seen at each dimension base structure factor organization, certainly that principal have done effort efficiency, clear design, coordination and useful good and exactly power source, so that relation organization could supported the management school. Since could be sure that organization structure have done.

Management organization SMP Terbuka Tulip at Malang Region with structure organization that principal have done for efficiency dimension was job description with vice and given confidential and full responsible, done discipline and procedure with clear. This job description have not done only vice, but teacher/tutor, treasure, adminitartion and student as its each job.

Principal have done and always at the visi, misi, school as the model so as the real role, used the discipline, as the "*softcopy*" and "*hardcopy*" data file, noted and booked, bill proved and with excellent reported, discipline and regular. From coordination dimension principal with responsible, confidential, task vice, teacher/tutor, treasure and administration its purposed to make easily coordination and done it step by step. This thing impact at the useful power source, because all the power source to be excellent. Concept education constant average so difficulty to arrange it. Prysor-Jones (dalam Suryadi dan Tilaar, 1994:29)

All phenomena that organization Structure base factor struktur organisasi could seen from each dimension, certainly that principal have done many efficiency effort, clear design, coordination and useful good and exactly power source, so that organization relation could supported the management school. So that be surely organization structure have done with good and exactly.

Finally all the proposition known that the principal as a leader at this school have done anykind of the management that supported in each its action, seen from its communication attitude effort, power source and organization structure that have done with excellent. (UNESCO ASPnet School).

Management organizatian SMP Terbuka Mawar at Malang Region with organization structure factor that principal have done for efficiency dimension was the clea job description vice, made be funcsional the task to the vice with given confidential and full responsible, done dicipline with clear, and made the right responsible design at the procedural. As the principal have not done visi, misi school as model that purpose for eliminate the fault, done dicipline, noted and booked, bill proved and made a good report, and regular, but all practical have not done. Principal coordination dimension with given responsible, confidential, task to the vice, teacher/tutor, treasure and administration was that made the purpose easily coordination and done step by step. This thing impact to the useful power source, because all the power source have not as its function.

From all the phenomena organization structure factor base could seen to each dimension, certainly that principal have done anykind efficiency effort, used the clear design, done coordination and useful power source with a good and exactly, although have not yet ability, not exactly and that management school supported. So could surely that organization structure have not yet done.

3. Development Power Source Management at the Open Junior High School (SMP Terbuka) Teratai, Tulip and Mawar at the Malang Region

Development power source management SMP Terbuka Teratai at Malang Region with power source factor could seen from the teacher/tutor invented not enough for any lesson, so that principal could not made policy to take several teacher/tutor for making a permanent teacher/

tutor that have relevance skill as the school was needed, said to the teacher/tutor active to the academic activity, given informative technology at their room, made the a group sitting as their lesson so that could discussion, given permit and easily to the teacher/tutor done sminar activity, training etc.

For its infrastructure school that supported principal management till now still repaired and build sequence athletic; mosque and its all facility comfortable; a health classroom learning, comfortable and with informative technology, science laboratory (physics, chemical and biology), library, multi-media room and computer room. Principal have prepared all the maintenance infrastructure, so that the instrument constantly its condition with given laboratory, technician, pointed teacher/tutor a responsible and operation discipline procedure. Principal have done effort management school with full attention. Financed and source cost for this school only budget from the school committee, from center government and region, generating income and from sponsor at a special time. Funding of the school have other source only at the budget and enough for its cash-flow. The budget of this school was used good enough with its needed and rational, priority scale financed, invoice bought, procedural and that have agreement fom principal and school conmittee. Sometimes principal not discipline useful the financed.

Anykind principal have done effort comunication management, anykind action that reach the goal, needed concrete, so each school management could done with excellent. The school problem power source have done with creative, objective and safety as the formal or nonformal. Surely that all aspect and dimension integrated with principal have done many power source with good at this school and exactly supported against school management. GSTaven@cbe.ab.ca.

Development power source have done management SMP Terbuka Tulip at the Malang Region with power source factor could seen from teacher/tutor as power source dimension invented not enough for any lesson, so that principal have taken policy with received several teacher/tutor, and function back that the teacher/tutor have pension for class have not its teacher/tutor, effort received the teacher/tutor have a relevance skill that as the school was needed and its experience, given permit and financed the teacher/tutor continue its study, given permit and the teacher/tutor followed seminar activity with easily, training etc.

Principal infrastructure facility school that supported a good management sequence athletic, mosque and the health classroom for learning, and informative technology, science laboratorium (physics, chemical and biology), library, multi-media classroom and computer classroom always repaired it. Institution by Principal have cared all infrastructure, so that the instrument always at the good condition, given facility technician, and its strong procedure used that discipline and responsible.

Source cost of this school onlu from the budget and financed from the government centre, region and institution, the cash-flow of this school enough. The useful budgeting very good because rational and as a needed, priority scale as budgeting with invoice bought, procedural and must have agreement from institution and principal.

Power source problem at this school enough good, objective, safe, good and formal or nonformal. So that certainly all the aspect and dimension, principal have done with good at this school and the management very supported.

Development management power source SMP Terbuka Mawar at Malang Region have seen with power source factor from the teacher/tutor invented still less its lesson, so that principal have taken policy with received several teacher/tutor, since each teacher/tutor not overlapping to teach. The teacher/tutor'honor effort to be a permanent teacher/tutor that have relevance skill as the school'need, sometimes given permit and easily to the teacher/tutor done its seminar activity, training and continue its study.

For facility physic infrastructure school that supported management principal till now still repaired and build sequence athletic, mosque and the health classroom for learning, and informative technology, science laboratorium (physics, chemical and biology) that dirty, library uninterested, multi-media room and computer room that simple. Principal not care the infrastructure not facility for laborer, technician, but received teacher/tutor that given responsible to care, although constant supported with useful procedure.

Source financed this school only from budget school committee, from the government centre, region and institution, the cash-flow of this school enough. The useful budgeting very good because rational and as a needed, priority scale as budgeting with invoice bought, procedural and must have agreement from institution and principal.

Sometimes principal not discipline in useful the financed. Principal several effort have done with management communication, action, needed concrete, projection, so each management school could done with good. Problem power source this school done not creative, objective and safe as formal or nonformal. So could be sure that all dimension and aspect that integrated with power source principal have done many, but not optimal and not to support management school.

4. **Management Audit System at the Open Junior High School (SMP Terbuka) Teratai, Tulip and Mawar at the Malang Region**

Management audit system SMP Terbuka Teratai at the Malang Region with audit factor seen from source dimension, principal have done direct and said the message management effort to the teacher/tutor via anykind, announcement at the teacher/tutor room, official meeting with loudspeaker, and with a letter. From dimension message, usually message management said as soon as and principal'principle never to suspend, its source from fact that obvious, with accurate and its message not far from the hope visi, misi. From media dimension, message said via loudspeaker, announcement at blackboard in the teacher/tutor room, SMS although not yet all, discuss non-formal with the same teacher/tutor, but not used *e-mail*. From dimension receiver message, They are known and respond far about righteousness and message. (Schawandt & Halpen, 1988:19)

Anykind effort that have done with anyway, as its any action so the message they said real could be known by the teacher/tutor with any respond to all and good. If principal said the message with common, individual and from loudspeaker, electronic and discuss. E-mail not yet used, because every teacher/tutor have not *"address e-mail"* although approach with formal or non-formal. So that be surely have many ways to say the management have done by the principal so could be received with conventional not with electronic and audit that have done real supported the management school. (Raka Joni, 1989).

Management audit system SMP Terbuka Tulip at the Malang Region with audit factor be seen from source dimension, principal have done said direct and the management message effort to the teacher/tutor with anyway, although announcement speaking and blackboard at teacher/tutor room and official meeting with loudspeaker. From message dimension, usually have said as soon as and principal'principle never to suspend, its source from fact that obvious, with accurate and its message not far from the hope visi, misi. From media dimension, message said via loudspeaker, announcement at blackboard in the teacher/tutor room, SMS although not yet all, discuss non-formal with the same teacher/tutor, but not used *e-mail*. From dimension receiver message, They are known and respond far about righteousness and message.

Anykind effort that have done with anyway, as its any action so the message they said real could be known by the teacher/tutor with any respond to all and good. If principal said the message with common, individual and from loudspeaker, electronic and discuss. E-mail not yet used, because every teacher/tutor have not *"address e-mail"* although approach with formal or non-formal. So that be surely have many ways to say the management have done by the principal so could be received with conventional not with electronic and audit that have done real supported the management school. (University of Nottingham, 2002)

Management audit system SMP Terbuka Mawar at the Malang Region with audit factor be seen from source dimension, principal have done said direct and the management message effort to the teacher/tutor with anyway, although announcement speaking and blackboard at teacher/tutor room and official meeting with loudspeaker. From message dimension, usually have said as soon as and principal'principle never to suspend, its source from fact that obvious, with accurate and its message not far from the hope visi, misi. From media dimension, message said via loudspeaker, announcement at blackboard in the teacher/tutor room, SMS although not yet all, discuss non-formal with the same teacher/tutor, but not used *e-mail*. From dimension receiver message, They are known and respond far about righteousness and message.

Anykind effort that have done with anyway, as its any action so the message they said real could be known by the teacher/tutor with any respond to all and good. If principal said the message with common, individual and from loudspeaker, electronic and discuss. E-mail not yet used, because every teacher/tutor have not *"address e-mail"* although approach with formal or non-formal. So that be surely have many ways to say the management have done by the principal so could be received with conventional not with electronic and audit that have done real supported the management school.

From the data that could be invented each to its school, that there are several things could be found as the conclusion spectacular when principal have done the condition of management school as the next.

a. Be seen from management school at the three SMP Terbuka impact against academic prestige, extra curricular and self-develop. That three of this SMP Terbuka were as the same favorite school, community trusted and prestige at the Malang Region so that many the parent of student have choosen because uniqueness and the most of the school.

b. Be seen from the three of SMP Terbuka above, that if principal have seen a quality in management school were (1) SMP terbuka Teratai Malang; (2) SMP Terbuka Tulip Malang; (3) SMP Terbuka Mawar Malang. Condition management school that quality would impact at the prestige school, and each school have most and less at SMP Terbuka Teratai different with SMP Terbuka Tulip, and if both of them compared with SMP Terbuka Mawar sure would different one to another.

c. Principal leadership as at SMP terbuka Teratai its condition management school more in itself leadership style as bureaucracy with its initiative, creative and high innovative, with supported and authority *"concept skills, operational skills and human skills"* that *smart*. Different with SMP Terbuka Tulip principal have done with leadership style as bureaucracy institution that sel-confidence and no comment outside of its responsible and authority that integrated with institution responsible. This things only to manage safety for its institution. SMP Terbuka Mawar principal'leadership style bureaucracy with not clear only done the management as its-self, and believed at the irrational that for its-self or its group.

d. Style at the SMP Terbuka Teratai principal have effort the condition management school more at the professional basic so principal more in creation for advancing the development school. Different with SMP Terbuka Tulip more effort at the role and rational that for normally, so that principal difficult for advancing the development school. Style at the

SMP Terbuka Mawar effort toward more to "rational and irrational," so principal needed a long time for advancing its school because unclear and so lately in action. Principal could be so tired and maybe would be frustration and ill at last give up.

e. Seen the term of responsible from the three school: style at SMP Terbuka Teratai would appeared concept "our responsible," advanced or not the school as responsible together between principal, teacher/tutor, staff, student, government, and "*stakeholders*" that integrated. Different with at SMP Terbuka Tulip would appeared concept "my responsible," that advanced of this school very depend at the leadership principal, as the institution believer. Style at SMP Terbuka Mawar would appeared concept "your responsible," that advanced or not this school depend who is as the principal.

f. Seen from responsible that appeared term for the three school. *The first*, with characteristic at SMP Terbuka Teratai that principal have seen the responsible to whom done the management school was a "message" that must done with excellent and ready heart. *Second*, different with characteristic as at SMP Terbuka Tulip that responsible of the principal where have given as "favour" that must done with excellent and ready heart. *Third*, would be more different with characteristic as at SMP Terbuka Mawar that responsible of the principal at their-self as "message" that must done with high conscious.

CHAPTER V
Closed

This Chapter described about Conclusion, Implication, and Suggestions as the next.

A. Conclusion.

From all the data and result analysis data at each site with analysis research multi-sites about "Management open Junior High School during the nine year compulsory education program" with study multi-sites SMP Terbuka Teratai, SMP Terbuka Tulip and SMP Terbuka Mawar at the Malang Region.

1. School Planning about management at the three Sites SMP Terbuka at the Malang Region.

Management school effort at SMP Terbuka principal and teacher/tutor that have done management planning have confirmed by school climated, made and easily relation one with another with ready heart to do it. Teacher/tutor have wanted, ability, and high commitment in management school planning, that could made management school with effective.

Principal have done with professional and proportional to school visi, and misi, with open and guard prestige school as the formal, able made functional, discipline and responsible.

2. Organization Management at the three Sites SMP Terbuka at the Malang Region.

Structure organization management at the SMP Terbuka that principal have done with simple, effective and efficiency organization, creative, principal, vice, teacher/tutor with clear job description and responsible.

Managed as the standard reference, visi, misi school and budget, coordinated organization with made a good procedure and organization communication with a good responsible functional.

Organization have done its-self because with consciously from each teacher/tutor, principal as a leader that have a *power* because there are supported from the teacher/tutor and staff at the school.

3. Development Power Source Management at the three Sites SMP Terbuka at the Malang Region.

Development power source effort management that have done at the SMP Terbuka principal have done made training, lokarya, seminar, reacher, discussion in and out of the school and made the same lesson group at the teacher/tutor rooms.

If humanity source with quantity and quality have balance, then would occurred acceleration and success in management school.

Facility with complete instrument were prepared at school would given positive impact against acceleration known the technology that build self-confidence to the teacher/tutor at the school, but with quality would impact against to reform creative level and innovation each person at the management school.

Implementation the management school supported with a good finance management, so that the education would be advanced and good character. And power source that prepared at the school have could used as the optimal by the principal, teacher, and student, that would good impacted against the quality support and done at the management school.

4. Management Audit System at the three Sites SMP Terbuka at Malang region.

Effort audit management audit system at the SMP Terbuka that have done by the principal school at the good environmental school and attentively social, so that implementation the management school would more effective and good. Management audit school that effective would happened if supported by source information direct that could responsibility, good from skill in said, reference that supported information as direct, although that accurated in the right level and could believed at the credibility. The warm messaged, from the clear fact, careful with not far from the vision and mission that be hoped. Media that used as much, made easily to said the information and that true representative and for the receiver believed have represent ordered that would be said.

Implementation management school at the three SMP Terbuka impacted against taken academic prestige, extra curriculer and self-develop. That the three SMP Terbuka this was together as the favorite school, be believed by community and prestige at Malang region so many the parents of student needed with any more and unique each that school. The three SMP Terbuka above, that if be seen quality each principal at the management school there was (1) SMP terbuka Teratai Malang; (2) SMP Terbuka Tulip Malang; (3) SMP Terbuka Mawar Malang. Condition management school that quality would impacted at the good quality school, and each school have more and less. SMP Terbuka Teratai different with SMP Terbuka Tulip, and if the two be compared with SMP Terbuka Mawar certainly far would different one the others. Principal leader'style as at the SMP terbuka Teratai more exactly if condition management school that implementation by principal with leader style as government bureaucracy with the high initiative, creative and innovative, with have supported a good concept skills, operational skills and human skills and smart. Differently with as at SMP Terbuka Tulip style if principal implementation with leader style as bureaucracy institution that self-condifence and no comment out of responsible and authorize at main things that integrated wuth institution responsible. This thing metaphor as film-star that only done and safe-guard for own institution. Therefore for at SMP Terbuka Mawar principal leader style that as a government bureaucracy that did not clear its mind only orientation at its own, implementation management as its own, and believed at the thins irrational that for himself or their group. Style as at SMP Terbuka Teratai principal efforted implementation school mnanagement condition more orientation at the base "professional and scientific," so that principal more Could advanced development its school creation. Different with style as at SMP Terbuka Tulip more effort stress to basic "rule and rational" that done as normally, so that principal not usually and limited in development the school advanced. And at SMP Terbuka Mawar style with efforted that toward stress more at the basic "rational and irrational" So the principal felt lately and needed a long time for advance the school. Responsible that appeared for the three school: for at SMP Terbuka Teratai style would appeared concept "our responsible," that advanced or not the school as responsible together between principal, teacher/tutor, staff, student, government and stakeholders that integrated. Different with at SMP Terbuka Tulip style would appered concept "my responsible," that advance of the school depend on of the leader that principal as institution believer. And at SMP Terbuka Mawar style would appeared concept "your responsible," that advanced or not the school was depended to who that as a principal. Seen from the responsible that must be front appeared term for the three school. *first*, with characteristic at SMP Terbuka Teratai that a principal seen the responsible that have given to someone for implementation management school was as "message" that must be done with care, good and full-heart. *Second*, different with characteristic as at SMP Terbuka Tulip that principal seen responsible that have given to himself was as "grace" that must be done with good as soul-call. *Third*, would different again with characteristic as at SMP Terhbuka Mawar that principal responsible to himself as "message" that must be done during this time till have awared himself that high for repenting.

B. Research Implication

Implication and this research invented included two things, that theorist implication and practical implication. Theorist Implication relation with it contribution yes for developing education management theories and pratical implication that integrated with contribution research invented against implementation management school.

1. Theories Implication

Theorist implication this research integrated with planning management school as the theory, this research have been awared that relation between planing management school could not separated both of its as same as the urgent and each supported always dynamics development. At once this research'result have limited although from its methodology or study as deeply about relation between factor that would be research, although as common could given theorist implication agreed with management and school organization, also coherency with quality and school efective in reaching the gol and target management school.

(Muhadjir, 2004:43), education management as efforted for social problem solution to be social problem for community on justiced and prosperity. (Cooper, 2004:3) said that policy as process politics where have be needed, gol and intensity that have done in objective view, law and program.

Study for the next that integrated with application and development management power source must be started with process reresearch at the management, also the target and aim. Managed Management education done school management, target and aim into strategy and operational management, and researched how have operational management? That have communication to managed management, power source have been prepared and useful, system and build the job description with implementation directly and development to competence. The next, research how to manage the management audit system education, and research more about the result quality and quantity, so that quality output as competence technician, managerial, attitude, skill, relevance quality output with needed, efficiency in education management.

(Tilaar, 1997:151) said "education have managed and function for teaching each citizen, and preparing power that have characteristic be needed for the industry-field, not as a main responsible."

All of that in contexts education managemen, that formulated, determination, management with outcomes. Theorist implication more the next, that where was laid its results and failure school management implementation? What was formulated and determination or at itself management process?

(Buchori, 2001:7) said that each nation where true needed to prepare himself for the future, must be born to do the changes at the education system, although at the formal education or non-formal education.

2. Practical Implication

As macro for formulating and determination school management needed to socialization more professional again, so that each managed could received message management with a good and not uncertain about it. In the future could be hoped to manage and give input and respond accommodate to be material balanced in formulating management that the future.

And as mikro as the next; *First,* planing school at the staff for managing each school management at a good needed. So that planning to care or to increase needed our supported development system and sat the right and good teacher/tutor. Principal neede to create climate school that conducive so that could done the management that teacher/tutor included at the formulate managed management and be hoped their as proactive to follow and give input at the school management operasional that its mean.

Second, managed organization that there are have done with a good unless at SMP Terbuka Mawar not yet at its function as be hoped, although constantly needed to arrange a good job system and procedure so that coordination between principal with the teacher/tutor good as internal or external could be increased. Principal needed to arrange standard operational procedure each school, so that could be happened fragmentation elimination.

Third, development power source managed management that have be prepared to need a better planning, useful and development, so that supported the effective and efficiency managed management. Each principal must efforted to make teacher/tutor surely done management reformation for the school future living. Conceling activities supervision learning, training and others felt very useful by all stakeholders. So that relation between principal with teacher/tutor as priority and continuously needed to increase relation functional used to increase again extension service as sustained, so could be reached to increase a good job. Useful result research needed supported by received teacher/tutor, so that between principal with teacher/tutor have standard operational procedure that clear in selection teacher/tutor that needed as each skill. Selection system managed to select a new teacher/tutor have a target for increasing quality teacher/tutor. Concept development test material and system determination the pass examination that principal have done, needed to be know to each teacher/tutor. Test managed or selection needed a good cooperation between principal, unit test managed that have been pointed and prepared the place for testing. So that test managed could happened with good and reached target that have needed.

Fourth, management audit system that relation with increased competence teacher/tutor at each school have audited to all management manged, but the management have not yet uniform perception by all management managed. Principal must be increased message quality that said to teacher/tutor from understanding *"what, why, who, when, where, and how"* about increased management competence teacher/tutor that means so to be more clear. Beside that each principal needed formulation strategies steps in increased effective communication management to all teacher/tutor. Henceforth be hoped teacher/tutor as proactive given feedback for perfecting message substance that be said their each principal. Management managed education needed to use this research result as the priced modal for developing school sustain. Would be better, if management managed education needed supported across school in doing and used modal that have been by stakeholders or with model transfer rotation as that have done at this last-day education service office at Malang region. This thing could to be also as efforted managed and with academic development teacger/tutor to be more interested. Henceforth management managed education with model regular or entrus needed to start and managed soon. Principal and teacher/tutor must be effort to increase quality process leraning that relation with management school, integrated with focus material that be said to student task, the power practical that competence and prepared material teaching that be needed as condition at the field. Be hoped Education Service could be sat a new teacher/tutor as with it competence that their having, so that could managed task and function as optimal

C. SUGGESTION

The basic of all analysis, research suggestion could used with hoped and benefit to:

5. For government Malang Region, in this thing education service at Malang region specially government instance that integrated with basic education as of nine year compulsory education of open junior high school at Malang region, this research invented could considered as one of foundation or input at done monitoring and evaluation or assessment against management managed of nine year compulsory education of open junior high school each a far region. with thus could done to repaire actions and development toward that more good so reached the target as with membership school hoping, community and government.

6. For Education Service Province and Excuting ministry in science development, this research result could hoped to be input for ascertain the policy more advanced and development education basic for nine year.

7. For Principal, specially SMP Terbuka at Malang region, this research result as material input for monitoring and evaluation against the management of nine year compulsory education of open junior high school so that could be increased in reaching that maximal target policy program of nine year compulsory education of open junior high school.

8. For others research, be hoped could to be inspiration for researh and scientific task and could be considered as material reference for that wanted to do sustain research with used approached design as the same research, and/or approached the different research.

DAFTAR RUJUKAN

Abdullah. 2004. *Professional Development for SD Teacher Through School Cluster, Teacher in Indonesia Their Education, Training and Struggle and Secondary Education.* Jakarta: Ministry of Nasional Education of The Republic Indonesia.

Achmady, Z.A. 1994. *Kebijakan Publik dan Pembangunan.* Malang: IKIP MALANG.

Alberta, C. 2006. *Terry Fox Junior High School has been a national accredited UNESCO ASPnet School.* (online) (ASPnet) diakses tanggal 15 Juli 2010.

Anderson, J. E. 1979. *Public Policy Making.* New York: Holt, Rinehart and Winston.

Arie, P. 1988. "*Planning Learning.*" Harvard Business Review. March – April, pp 70 – 74.

Bogdan, R.C. dan Biklen, S.K. 1998. *Qualitative Research for Education: an Introduction to Theory and Methods.* Needham Heigths, MA: Allyn & Bacon A Viacom Company.

Buchori, M. 2001. *Transformasi Pendidikan.* Jakarta: Pustaka Sinar Harapan.

Burhanuddin. 2002. *Manajemen Pendidikan: Wacana, Proses dan Aplikasinya di Sekolah.* Malang: Universitas Negeri Malang.

Cooper, B.S. 2004. *Better Policy Better School, Theories and Application.* Boston: Pearson Education.

Creswell, J.W. 2005. *Education Research Planning, Conducting, and Evaluating: Quantitative and Qualitatif Research.* New Jersey: Upper Saddle River.

David, T. GST. Aven. 2010. *Old Junior/Senoir High School.* (online) (http://www.isflst.ca. dan davidthian@shaw.ca. dan GSTaven@cbe.ab.ca.) diakses 17 Juli 2010.

Departemen Pendidikan dan Kebudayaan. 1990. *Peraturan Pemerintah RI Nomor: 28 Tahun 1990 Tentang Pendidikan Dasar.* Jakarta: Departemen Pendidikan dan Kebudayaan.

Departemen Pendidikan dan Kebudayaan. 1992. *Pedoman Pelaksanaan Sistem SMP Terbuka.* Jakarta: Proyek Peningkatan Kebijaksanaan Operasional Pembangunan dan Pengorganisasian Departemen Pendidikan dan Kebudayaan.

Departemen Pendidikan dan Kebudayaan. 1993. *Keputusan Menteri Pendidikan dan Kebudayaan No. 54/U/1993 Tentang Sekolah Menengah Pertama (SMP).* Jakarta: Departemen Pendidikan dan Kebudayaan.

Departemen Pendidikan Nasional. 2003. *Undang-undang Nomor 20 Tahun 2003 Tentang Sistem Pendidikan Nasional.* Jakarta: Depdiknas.

Departemen Pendidikan Nasional. 2005. *Bahan Sosialisasi SMP Terbuka Dalam Rangka Penuntasan Wajib Wajib Belajar Pendidikan Dasar 9 Tahun.* Jakarta: Depdiknas.

Departemen Pendidikan Nasional. 2005. *Peraturan Pemerintah Republik Indonesia Nomor 19 Tahun 2005 Tentang Standar Nasional Pendidikan.* Jakarta: Depdiknas.

Departemen Pendidikan Nasional. 2005. *Petunjuk Operasional SMP Terbuka.* Jakarta: Direktorat Pembinaan Sekolah Menengah Pertama, Direktorat Jenderal Manajemen Pendidikan Dasar dan Menengah Depdiknas.

Departemen Pendidikan Nasional. 2005. *Petunjuk Pengelolaan TKB Mandiri.* Jakarta: Direktorat Pembinaan Sekolah Menengah Pertama, Direktorat Jenderal Manajemen Pendidikan Dasar dan Menengah Depdiknas.

Departemen Pendidikan Nasional. 2006. *Peraturan Menteri Pendidikan Nasional RI Nomor: 35 Tahun 2006 Tentang Gerakan Nasional Percepatan Wajib Belajar 9 Tahun.* Jakarta: Depdiknas.

Departemen Pendidikan Nasional. 2006. *Rencana Strategis Departemen Pendidikan Nasional 2005-2009 Menuju Pembangunan Nasional Jangka Panjang 2025.* Jakarta: Depdiknas.

Departemen Pendidikan Nasional. 2007. *Pengembangan Bakat Non-Akademik: Pengembangan Kemampuan Manajerial.* Jakarta: Depdiknas.

Departemen Pendidikan Nasional. 2007. *Peraturan Menteri Pendidikan Nasional Republik Indonesia No. 19 Tahun 2007 Tentang Standar Pengelolaan Pendidikan Oleh Satuan Pendidikan Dasar dan Menengah.* Dalam Warta Hukum dan Perundang-undangan, Vol. 8, No. 3, Desember 2007:p. 19-35. Jakarta: Biro Hukum dan Organisasi Depdiknas.

Devlin, L. 1989. *"A Closer Look."* Canadian Journal of University Continuing Education. Vol.15. No. 1.pp 29 – 38.

Djojonegoro, W. 1996. *50 Tahun Perkembangan Pendidikan Indonesia.* Jakarta: Depdikbud.

Duke, D.L. & Canady, R.L. 1991. *School Policy.* New York: McGraw-Hill.

Dunn, W. 2000. *Pengantar Analisis Kebijakan Publik.* Penyunting Muhajir Darwin. Yogyakarta: Gadjah Mada University Press.

Fahrurroji, M. 2008. *Mengukur Keberhasilan Wajar Dikdas 9 Tahun dan Kesiapan Wajar Dikmen 12 Tahun yang Bermutu di Kota Samarinda.* www.mfahrurroji.blogspot.com, diakses tanggal 12 Agustus 2008.

Faisal, S. 2005. *Format-format Penelitian Sosial.* Jakarta: RajaGrafindo Persada.

Fattah, N. 2008. *Landasan Manajemen Pendidikan.* Bandung: Remaja Rosdakarya.

Georg, S. 1987. *"Strategic Control: A New Perspective.*: Academy of Management Review. January, pp 91 – 103.

Hodgetts, R. M. 1990. *Management Theory, Process, and Practice.* San Diego: Harcourt Brace Jovanovich, Publishers.

Ikatan Sarjana Pendidikan Indonesia (ISPI). 1995. *Pendidikan dan Prospeknya Terhadap Pembangunan Bangsa Dalam PJP II.* Jakarta. Ikatan Sarjana Pendidikan Indonesia (ISPI).

Instruksi Presiden RI. No. 1 Tahun 1994 tentang Wajib Belajar Pendidikan Dasar 9 Tahun. Jakarta: Sekretariat Negara RI.

Indonesia. 1997. *Ministry of Education and Culture Education Development Indonesia.* Jakarta.

Irawan, B. S. 2008. *Analisis Kebijakan Pertahanan.* www.buletinlitbangdephan.gi.id, diakses tanggal 13 Agustus 2008.

Jalal, Fasli dan Dedi Supriyadi (Ed.). 2001. *Reformasi Pendidikan Dalam Konteks Otonomi Daerah.* Yogyakarta: Adicita Karya Nusa.

Lincoln, YS & Guba EGL. 1985. *Naturalistic Inquiry.* Beverly Hill. CA: SAGE Publications, Inc.

Maisyaroh, dkk. (ed.). 2004. *Perspektif Manajemen Pendidikan Berbasis Sekolah.* Malang: Universitas Negeri Malang

Majelis Permusyawaratan Rakyat Republik Indonesia. 2006. *Panduan Pemasyarakatan Undang-undang Dasar Negara Republik Indonesia Tahun 1945.* Jakarta: Sekretariat Jenderal MPR RI.

Meyer, R. R. dan Greenwood, E. 1984. *Rancangan Penelitian Kebijakan Sosial.* Jakarta: Rajawali.

Miarso, Yusufhadi. 1985. *Suatu Model Teknologi Pendidikan Untuk Pemerataan Kesempatan Pendidikan di Indonesia.* Yogyakarta: Adicita Karya Nusantara

Miarso, Yusufhadi. 2007. *Menyemai Benih Teknologi Pendidikan.* Jakarta, Kencana.

Miles, M.B. dan Huberman, A.M. 1992. *Qualitative Data Analysis: a Sourcebook of New Methods.* London: Sage Publications.

Moleong, L.J. 2005. *Metodologi Penelitian Kualitatif.* Bandung: Rosdakarya.

Muhajir, N. 2004. *Metodologi Penelitian Kebijakan dan Evaluasi Research* (*Integrasi Penelitian, Kebijakan dan Perencanaan*). Yogyakarta: Rake Sarasin.

Mulyana, D. 2008. *Metodologi Penelitian Kualitatif.* Bandung: Remaja Rosdakarya.

Nazir, A. S. 2002. *Knowledge Management.* FAQ. Buletin: Department of Information Systems, FSKSM, UTM.

Patton, M. Q. 1990. *Qualitative Evaluation and Research Methods.* Second Edition, Newbury Park: SAGE Publications Inc.

Patton, M. Q. 2006. *Metode Evaluasi Kualitatif* (*How To Use Qualitative Methods in Evaluation*). Yogyakarta: Pustaka Pelajar.

Patricia, N. F. 1987. "*Communation Skills Training for Selected Supervisors.*" Training and Develop Journal, July, pp 67 – 70.

Prasetyo. 2007. *Ceramah ISO 9001:2000* (online) (http://prasetyo brawijaya.ac.id/agu04.htm#iso)

Pemerintah Kota Malang. 2009. *Profil Pendidikan Kota Malang Tahun 2009.* Malang: Pemerintah Kota Malang.

Purwanto, N. 2006. *Administrasi dan Supervisi Pendidikan.* Bandung: Remaja Rosdakarya.

Peter M. 1956. *Bueaucracy in Modern Society.* New York: Random House, pp 28 – 33.

Rahardjo, D. 1997. *Relevansi Iptek Profetik Dalam Pembangunan Masyarakat Madani.* Academika, Vol. 01, Th. XV, hal. 17-24.

Raka J, 1989. *Pendidikan Profesional Guru,* Malang: Universitas Negeri Malang.

Randall, S. H. 2010. *The Importance of The High School Junior Year.* (online) (http://www.quintcareer.com). Diakses tanggal 17 Juli 2010.

Rochaety, E, dkk. 2005. *Sistem Informasi Manajemen Pendidikan.* Jakarta: Bumi Aksara.

Ross, T. 1998. *A Principal's Intterruption; Time Loss or Time Gained?* International Journal Education Management. 12 June, pp 244 – 249.

Samanan, A. 2008. *Analisis Kebijakan SD-SMP Satu Atap Dalam Percepatan Program Wajib Belajar 9 Tahun di Kabupaten Jember.* Tesis tidak diterbitkan. Malang: Program Studi Magister Kebijakan dan Pengembangan Pendidikan Program Pascasarjana Universitas Muhammadiyah Malang.

Sarwono, J. 2003. *Strategi Melakukan Penelitian di Internet.* World Wide Web: http://js.unikom.ac.id

Schawandt, T.A. dan Halpern, E.S. 1988. *Linking Auditing and Metaevaluation: Enhancing Qualityin Applied Research.* Newbury Park, Beverly Hills, London, New Delhi: Sage Publication.

School Accountability Report Card. Reported for School Year. 2009 – 2010. Published during 2010 – 2011. (online) (http://www.cde.ca.gov/ta/ac/sa/.) diakses 19 Juli 2010.

Sergiovanni, T. J. 1987. *"Symbolism in Leadership: What Great Leaders Know that ordinary Ones do not,"* Paper Present to the Institute of Education Administration. Geelong, Victoria.

Sidi, I. D. 2001. *Menuju Masyarakat Pembelajar (Menggagas Paradigma Baru Pendidikan).* Jakarta: Paramadina.

Sonhadji, K. H. A. 1994. *Teknis Pengumpulan dan Analisis Data dalam Penelitian Kualitatif.* Malang: Kalimasada.

Stuart, W. 2008. *A Review of the Implementation of nine years Universal Basic Education,* USAID, Indonesia

Sudijarto. 1997. *Memantapkan Kinerja Sistem Pendidikan Nasional dalam Menyiapkan Manusia Indonesia Memasuki Abad ke-21.* Bandung: Rosdakarya.

Suharsaputra, U. *Pemerataan Pendidikan.* www.lappkipnikng.com, diakses tanggal 12 Agutus 2008.

Sukmadinata, N. S. 2007. *Pendidikan Dasar.* Jakarta: Universitas Pendidikan Indonesia.

Sukriswandari, N. 2005. *Analisa Singkat Perkembangan Pelaksanaan Program Penuntasan Wajar 9 Tahun yang Bermutu.* Pelangi Pendidikan II: hal. 57.

Supandi, A. S. 1988. *Kebijaksanaan dan Keputusan Pendidikan.* Jakarta: P2LTPK.

Supriadi, D. 2004. *Membangun Bangsa Melalui Pendidikan.* Bandung: Remaja Rosdakarya.

Suryadi, A. dan Tilaar, H.A.R. 1994. *Analisis Kebijakan pendidikan: Suatu Pengantar.* Bandung: Rosda Karya.

Sutopo, H.B. 2003. Pengumpulan dan Pengolahan Data Dalam Penelitian Kualitatif. Dalam buku *Metodologi Penelitian Kualitatif: Tinjauan Teoritis dan Praktis.* Editor Masykuri Badri, dkk. Malang: Lembaga Penelitian Universitas Islam Malang.

Syafaruddin. 2002. *Manajemen Mutu Terpadu dalam Pendidikan: Konsep. Strategi dan Aplikasi.* Jakarta: Grasindo.

Tilaar, H.A.R. 1997. *Pengembangan Sumber Daya Manusia Dalam Era Globalisasi, Visi, Misi dan Program Aksi Pendidikan dan Pelatihan Menuju 2020.* Jakarta: Grasindo.

Tilaar, H.A.R. 2002. *Membenahi Pendidikan Nasional.* Jakarta: Rineka Cipta.

University of Nottingham. *University Quality Handbook 2002/2005.* Download. 24 Agustus 2010. Pk. 10.00.

Yin,. R. K. 1984. *Case Study: Design and Method.* Thousand Oaks, C.A: Sage Publications, Inc.

APPENDIX

OBSERVATION SHEET FORMAT

Work Unit   : Open Jnuior High School (SMP Terbuka)
Date Interview   :.....................
Time   :....................
Placed   :...................
Source Data   :......................(L/P)
Research   : Soetyono Iskandar.

Focus	Item			Question	Information
	Factor	Dimension	Aspect		
1.	Planned	What Attitude that must be done, ability for doing motivation and desire		1. How good attitude was done ? What action could support to execute the management? 2. How good was ability could support to execute the management? 3. How good was motivation and desire could support to execute the management	1........................ .... 2........................ .... 3........................ ....
	Organization	Efficiency, used model, coordination, benefit source power .		How good quality efficiency, used model, coordination, benefit source power could support the management	1. Efficiency .... 2. Used Model .... 3. Coordination .... 4. Benefit source power ....

OBSERVATION SHEET FORMAT

Work Unit   : Open Jnuior High School (SMP Terbuka)
Date Interview   :.......................
Time   :.......................
Placed   :.......................
Source Data   :.......................(L/P)
Research   : Soetyono Iskandar.

Focus	Item			Questions	Information
	Factor	Dimension	Aspect		
1.	Development	Human, physic, instrument and financial	Quantity and quality	How good quantity and quality SDM, physic, instrument and financial could support the management	1. SDM a. Quantity ....….. ....….. b. Quality ....….. ....….. 2. Physic, instrument, a. Quantity ....….. ....….. b. Quality ....….. ....….. 3. Financial a. Quantity ....….. ....….. b. Quality ....….. ....…..

OBSERVATION SHEET FORMAT

Work Unit   : Open Jnuior High School (SMP Terbuka)
Date Interview   :.......................
Time   :.......................
Placed   :.......................
Source Data   :.......................(L/P)
Research   : Soetyono Iskandar.

Focus	Item			Pertanyaan	Informasi
	Factor	Dimensi on	Aspect		
1.	Audit System	Message	Renew, transformational, clarity, accurate, consistency	How good quality renew, transformational, clarity, accurate, consistency could support the management	a. Renew .... b. Transformational .... c. Clarity .... d. Accurate .... e. consistency ....
		Media	Preparedness, easilyness, Representative	How good quality preparedness, easilyness, representative coul support the management	a. Preparedness .... b. Easilyness .... c. Representative ....
		Received message		How good quality received message could support the management	Believed/not, reason: ....

148

OBSERVATION RESULT EXAMPLE

Work Unit   : Open Jnuior High School (SMP Terbuka) Teratai
Date Interview   : 15 Juli 2010
Time   : 13 -15 Wita
Placed   : Teacher/tutor room
Source Data   : Drs. Arif Rahman (L)
Research   : Soetyono Iskandar.

Focus	Item			Pertanyaan	Informasi
	Factor	Dimension	Aspect		
1.	Planned	What attitude that must be done, ability the motivation and desire.		1.How good attitude was done? What must be done to support executed the management? 2.How good ability was done? So could support the management 3.How good was motivation and desire could support to execute the management?.	1.Seen from attitude dimention what principal have executed? Principal'attitude have efforted to do the managerial, that's abled to separate attitude for school and theirself; recreated strcture relationship with simply organization; have not known action special. Given serviced with fast, suitable, easi and satisfied but rational as the rule. 2. Principal ability managed this school have more than average ability that support the school management. Leadership have worked succeed with never postponement. 3.Seen from motivation dimension and desire *the big dreams.* Succed door with coordination, responsibility, to vice, teacher/tutor with their *job descrption.* To each their field.

OBSERVATION RESULT EXAMPLE

Work Unit   : Open Jnuior High School (SMP Terbuka) Teratai

Date Interview   : 15 Juli 2010

Time   : 13 -15 Wita

Placed   : Teacher/tutor room

Source Data   : Drs. Arif Rahman (L)

Research   : Soetyono Iskandar.

Focus	Item			Questions	Information
	Factor	Dimension	Aspect		
1.	Organization	Efficiency, used model.		How good quality efficiency, used model, coordination and benafit source.	1.Efficiency at this school function vice actually as their function. Principal as coordinator only and have given full responsibility at the jobscription. 2.Used Model responsibility have given to them with standard operational executed that clear even with individual sanction as at the policy and at the school vision and mission. 3. Coordination Principal have coordinated response to vice and teacher/tutor about "*job description*," so that each known their task. Principal "*to manage*" and strived, controlled, and evaluation that response. 4. Benefit source power; principal have tried with all potence source power included believed to their teacher/tutor.

OBSERVATION RESULT EXAMPLE

Work Unit : Open Jnuior High School (SMP Terbuka) Teratai
Date Interview : 17 Juli 2010
Time : 13 -15 Wita
Placed : Teacher/tutor room
Source Data : Drs. Arif Rahman (L)
Research : Soetyono Iskandar.

Fous	Item			Question	Informasi
	Factor	Dimension	Aspect		
1.	Source power	Human physic, instrument and financial	Quantity and quality	How good quantity and qualitas SDM physic, instrument and financial could support to execute the school management.	1.SDM a. Quantity as Quantity the teacher/tutor at this school still less, if compared with totally student. But their responsibility, dedication, victim against school very high. b. Quality Principal'Qualitas, desire, ability, commitment to manage this school supported with leadership attitude constructive aseducated, skill, democracy. As quality as the teacher /tutor, administration still low. 2. Physic, instrument a. Quantitas as quantity at the school that supported learning infrastructure minimal, like classroom that big size and used AC. Laboratory science (physical, chemical, and biology), library, learning-media, and multy-media room (Informatica Technology), have prepared completed till sport infrastructure. b. Quality As quality facility physic and instrument that prepared at this school still in agood condition, reday foe use, specification still up to date, but have not maintannace, 3. Financial. a. Quantity As quantity not more all of from the budget source and fund from the government routine. b. Quality As quality this school not more than compared with others school that source from budget, but there are fund added "*generating income*" that could find money, so the impact at the "*cash flow*" financial this school seen health.

OBSERVATION RESULT EXAMPLE

Work Unit   : Open Jnuior High School (SMP Terbuka) Teratai
Date Interview   : 17 Juli 2010
Time   : 13 -15 Wita
Placed   : Teacher/tutor room
Source Data   : Drs. Arif Rahman (L)
Research   : Soetyono Iskandar.

Focus	Item			Questions	Information
	Factor	Dimension	Aspect		
1.	Audit System	Message	Renew, transformational, clarity, accurate, consistence	How good quality renew, transformational, clarity, accurate, consistence could support to execute the school management.	a.Renew Message that have said always warm or up to date b.Transformational Message that have said from the fact the actually. c.Clarity Message that have said that right objective. d.Accurate Message that have said with a good consideration, accurate, righteousness, discuss, observation, and that fact commitment. e.Consistence Message have as the school vision and mision.

OBSERVATION RESULT EXAMPLE

Work Unit   : Open Jnuior High School (SMP Terbuka) Teratai
Date Interview   : 17 Juli 2010
Time   : 13 -15 Wita
Placed   : Teacher/tutor room
Source Data   : Drs. Arif Rahman (L)
Research   : Soetyono Iskandar.

Focus	Item			Questions	Information
	Factor	Dimension	Aspect		
1.	Audit System	Media	Preparedness, easilyness and representative	How good quality prepared, easilyness and representative could support to execute the school management.	1.Preparedness Many media that have prepared 2.Easillyness Teacher/tutor easi could find media as support the school management. 3.Representative Media that used the right representative message that would say.

OBSERVATION RESULT EXAMPLE

Work Unit   : Open Jnuior High School (SMP Terbuka) Teratai
Date Interview : 17 Juli 2010
Time   : 13 -15 Wita
Placed   : Teacher/tutor room
Source Data   : Drs. Arif Rahman (L)
Research   : Soetyono Iskandar.

Focus	Item			Questions	Information
	Factor	Dimension	Aspect		
1.	Audit System	Received message		How good quality received message could support the school management.	Believed/not, reason: Teacher/tutor have not known what the principal desire? so that message could not know of them. Each receiver message the policy have theirself vision and mission.

INTERVIEW QUESTION LIST

A. Research question list

1. Pleading for information, how principal was reacted about the school management?
2. Pleading for information, how principal attitude when communication about the school management?
3. Pleading for information, how principal was cared orginality message that have said the communication at the school?
4. Pleading for information, how principal was cared a good level comunication?
5. Pleading for information, how the teacher/tutor was imaged a good source power as quantitative and qualitative at the school?
6. Pleading for information, what was the teacher/tutor seldom called and followed at the school training?
7. Pleading for information, how the teacher/tutor was used facility Informatica of Technology and instrument at the school?
8. Pleading for information, how principal attitude must be executed at the school?
9. Pleading for information, how principal ability was managed function and their job at the school?
10. Pleading for information, how principal was given motivation to their teacher/tutor at the school?
11. Pleading for information, how principal was worked optimal relationship between principal, vice, and teacher/tutor at the school?
12. Pleading for information, how principal was coordinated relationship between principal, vice and teacher/tutor at the school?

B. Aspect that have needed observation

1. Quality plannned
2. Quality organization

3. Quality development source power

4. Quality management Audit system

C. Data and material that needed to seek for

1. School document

2. School profile

3. Data/proved school prestation

4. Notulen result meeting was not as the secret

5. Several document problem integrated with school policy

INTERVIEW RESULT FORMAT

Work Unit   : Open Junior High School (SMP Terbuka)
Date Interview   :......................
Time   :......................
Placed   :......................
Source Data   :......................(L/P)
Research   : Soetyono Iskandar.

No	Data Source	Focus	Describes

INTERVIEW RESULT

Work Unit : Open Jnuior High School (SMP Terbuka)
Date Interview : 17 Juli 2010
Time : 13 -15 Wita
Placed : Teacher/tutor room
Source Data : Drs. Arif Rahman (L)
Research : Soetyono Iskandar.

No	Data Source	Focus	Describes
1.			The first we was introduced at the schoolboard and allof the staffs overthere. Principal always taught all of for this school, how and who? Always called for discussion, taught and to precede about school advanced. Everyday that integrated with serious, enjoy, sport together with all the teacher/tutor, like "*refreshing*" and eating together. As representative as teacher/tutor must be made this school advanced. Teacher/tutor seldom integrated at the computer training, internet, English language and "*e-learning,*" but have not abled, because full with their lesson teaching. Actually each teacher/tutor have a computer and their children could use computer, but I did not know, why?.... at last back as the former, as laugh ashamed.

INTERVIEW RESULT

Work Unit   : Open Jnuior High School (SMP Terbuka)
Date Interview   : 2010
Time   : .... Wita
Placed   : ....
Source Data   : ....
Research   : Soetyono Iskandar.

No	Data Source	Focus	Describes
1.			

INTERVIEW RESULT

Work Unit   : Open Jnuior High School (SMP Terbuka)
Date Interview   : ……….. 2010
Time   : ………. Wita
Placed   : ………………
Source Data   : ………………
Research   : Soetyono Iskandar.

No	Data Source	Focus	Describes
1.			

INTERVIEW RESULT

Work Unit   : Open Jnuior High School (SMP Terbuka)
Date Interview   : 2010
Time   : .... Wita
Placed   : ....
Source Data   : ....
Research   : Soetyono Iskandar.

No	Data Source	Focus	Describes
1.			

INTERVIEW RESULT

Work Unit   : Open Jnuior High School (SMP Terbuka)
Date Interview   : 2010
Time   : .... Wita
Placed   : ....
Source Data   : ....
Research   : Soetyono Iskandar.

No	Data Source	Focus	Describes
1.			